PHONE CALL LOG BOOK

DATE: TIME:	MESSAGE:
NAME:	
COMPANY:	
PHONE:	
EMAIL:	
IMPORTANCE: LOW ☐ MEDIUM ☐ HIGH ☐	CALLED ☐
DATE: TIME:	MESSAGE:
NAME:	
COMPANY:	
PHONE:	
EMAIL:	
IMPORTANCE: LOW ☐ MEDIUM ☐ HIGH ☐	CALLED ☐
DATE: TIME:	MESSAGE:
NAME:	
COMPANY:	
PHONE:	
EMAIL:	
IMPORTANCE: LOW ☐ MEDIUM ☐ HIGH ☐	CALLED ☐
DATE: TIME:	MESSAGE:
NAME:	
COMPANY:	
PHONE:	
EMAIL:	
IMPORTANCE: LOW ☐ MEDIUM ☐ HIGH ☐	CALLED ☐
DATE: TIME:	MESSAGE:
NAME:	
COMPANY:	
PHONE:	
EMAIL:	
IMPORTANCE: LOW ☐ MEDIUM ☐ HIGH ☐	CALLED ☐

DATE: **TIME:**	**MESSAGE:**
NAME:	
COMPANY:	
PHONE:	
EMAIL:	
IMPORTANCE: LOW ☐ **MEDIUM** ☐ **HIGH** ☐	**CALLED** ☐
DATE: **TIME:**	**MESSAGE:**
NAME:	
COMPANY:	
PHONE:	
EMAIL:	
IMPORTANCE: LOW ☐ **MEDIUM** ☐ **HIGH** ☐	**CALLED** ☐
DATE: **TIME:**	**MESSAGE:**
NAME:	
COMPANY:	
PHONE:	
EMAIL:	
IMPORTANCE: LOW ☐ **MEDIUM** ☐ **HIGH** ☐	**CALLED** ☐
DATE: **TIME:**	**MESSAGE:**
NAME:	
COMPANY:	
PHONE:	
EMAIL:	
IMPORTANCE: LOW ☐ **MEDIUM** ☐ **HIGH** ☐	**CALLED** ☐
DATE: **TIME:**	**MESSAGE:**
NAME:	
COMPANY:	
PHONE:	
EMAIL:	
IMPORTANCE: LOW ☐ **MEDIUM** ☐ **HIGH** ☐	**CALLED** ☐

	MESSAGE:
DATE: **TIME:**	
NAME:	
COMPANY:	
PHONE:	
EMAIL:	
IMPORTANCE: LOW ☐ **MEDIUM** ☐ **HIGH** ☐	**CALLED** ☐
DATE: **TIME:**	**MESSAGE:**
NAME:	
COMPANY:	
PHONE:	
EMAIL:	
IMPORTANCE: LOW ☐ **MEDIUM** ☐ **HIGH** ☐	**CALLED** ☐
DATE: **TIME:**	**MESSAGE:**
NAME:	
COMPANY:	
PHONE:	
EMAIL:	
IMPORTANCE: LOW ☐ **MEDIUM** ☐ **HIGH** ☐	**CALLED** ☐
DATE: **TIME:**	**MESSAGE:**
NAME:	
COMPANY:	
PHONE:	
EMAIL:	
IMPORTANCE: LOW ☐ **MEDIUM** ☐ **HIGH** ☐	**CALLED** ☐
DATE: **TIME:**	**MESSAGE:**
NAME:	
COMPANY:	
PHONE:	
EMAIL:	
IMPORTANCE: LOW ☐ **MEDIUM** ☐ **HIGH** ☐	**CALLED** ☐

DATE:	TIME:	MESSAGE:
NAME:		
COMPANY:		
PHONE:		
EMAIL:		
IMPORTANCE: LOW ☐ MEDIUM ☐ HIGH ☐		CALLED ☐

DATE:	TIME:	MESSAGE:
NAME:		
COMPANY:		
PHONE:		
EMAIL:		
IMPORTANCE: LOW ☐ MEDIUM ☐ HIGH ☐		CALLED ☐

DATE:	TIME:	MESSAGE:
NAME:		
COMPANY:		
PHONE:		
EMAIL:		
IMPORTANCE: LOW ☐ MEDIUM ☐ HIGH ☐		CALLED ☐

DATE:	TIME:	MESSAGE:
NAME:		
COMPANY:		
PHONE:		
EMAIL:		
IMPORTANCE: LOW ☐ MEDIUM ☐ HIGH ☐		CALLED ☐

DATE:	TIME:	MESSAGE:
NAME:		
COMPANY:		
PHONE:		
EMAIL:		
IMPORTANCE: LOW ☐ MEDIUM ☐ HIGH ☐		CALLED ☐

DATE: **TIME:**	**MESSAGE:**
NAME:	
COMPANY:	
PHONE:	
EMAIL:	
IMPORTANCE: LOW ▢ MEDIUM ▢ HIGH ▢	**CALLED** ▢
DATE: **TIME:**	**MESSAGE:**
NAME:	
COMPANY:	
PHONE:	
EMAIL:	
IMPORTANCE: LOW ▢ MEDIUM ▢ HIGH ▢	**CALLED** ▢
DATE: **TIME:**	**MESSAGE:**
NAME:	
COMPANY:	
PHONE:	
EMAIL:	
IMPORTANCE: LOW ▢ MEDIUM ▢ HIGH ▢	**CALLED** ▢
DATE: **TIME:**	**MESSAGE:**
NAME:	
COMPANY:	
PHONE:	
EMAIL:	
IMPORTANCE: LOW ▢ MEDIUM ▢ HIGH ▢	**CALLED** ▢
DATE: **TIME:**	**MESSAGE:**
NAME:	
COMPANY:	
PHONE:	
EMAIL:	
IMPORTANCE: LOW ▢ MEDIUM ▢ HIGH ▢	**CALLED** ▢

DATE: TIME:	MESSAGE:
NAME:	
COMPANY:	
PHONE:	
EMAIL:	
IMPORTANCE: LOW ☐ MEDIUM ☐ HIGH ☐	CALLED ☐

DATE: TIME:	MESSAGE:
NAME:	
COMPANY:	
PHONE:	
EMAIL:	
IMPORTANCE: LOW ☐ MEDIUM ☐ HIGH ☐	CALLED ☐

DATE: TIME:	MESSAGE:
NAME:	
COMPANY:	
PHONE:	
EMAIL:	
IMPORTANCE: LOW ☐ MEDIUM ☐ HIGH ☐	CALLED ☐

DATE: TIME:	MESSAGE:
NAME:	
COMPANY:	
PHONE:	
EMAIL:	
IMPORTANCE: LOW ☐ MEDIUM ☐ HIGH ☐	CALLED ☐

DATE: TIME:	MESSAGE:
NAME:	
COMPANY:	
PHONE:	
EMAIL:	
IMPORTANCE: LOW ☐ MEDIUM ☐ HIGH ☐	CALLED ☐

DATE: **TIME:**	**MESSAGE:**
NAME:	
COMPANY:	
PHONE:	
EMAIL:	
IMPORTANCE: LOW ☐ **MEDIUM** ☐ **HIGH** ☐	**CALLED** ☐
DATE: **TIME:**	**MESSAGE:**
NAME:	
COMPANY:	
PHONE:	
EMAIL:	
IMPORTANCE: LOW ☐ **MEDIUM** ☐ **HIGH** ☐	**CALLED** ☐
DATE: **TIME:**	**MESSAGE:**
NAME:	
COMPANY:	
PHONE:	
EMAIL:	
IMPORTANCE: LOW ☐ **MEDIUM** ☐ **HIGH** ☐	**CALLED** ☐
DATE: **TIME:**	**MESSAGE:**
NAME:	
COMPANY:	
PHONE:	
EMAIL:	
IMPORTANCE: LOW ☐ **MEDIUM** ☐ **HIGH** ☐	**CALLED** ☐
DATE: **TIME:**	**MESSAGE:**
NAME:	
COMPANY:	
PHONE:	
EMAIL:	
IMPORTANCE: LOW ☐ **MEDIUM** ☐ **HIGH** ☐	**CALLED** ☐

DATE: **TIME:**	**MESSAGE:**
NAME:	
COMPANY:	
PHONE:	
EMAIL:	
IMPORTANCE: LOW ☐ MEDIUM ☐ HIGH ☐	**CALLED ☐**
DATE: **TIME:**	**MESSAGE:**
NAME:	
COMPANY:	
PHONE:	
EMAIL:	
IMPORTANCE: LOW ☐ MEDIUM ☐ HIGH ☐	**CALLED ☐**
DATE: **TIME:**	**MESSAGE:**
NAME:	
COMPANY:	
PHONE:	
EMAIL:	
IMPORTANCE: LOW ☐ MEDIUM ☐ HIGH ☐	**CALLED ☐**
DATE: **TIME:**	**MESSAGE:**
NAME:	
COMPANY:	
PHONE:	
EMAIL:	
IMPORTANCE: LOW ☐ MEDIUM ☐ HIGH ☐	**CALLED ☐**
DATE: **TIME:**	**MESSAGE:**
NAME:	
COMPANY:	
PHONE:	
EMAIL:	
IMPORTANCE: LOW ☐ MEDIUM ☐ HIGH ☐	**CALLED ☐**

DATE:	TIME:	MESSAGE:
NAME:		
COMPANY:		
PHONE:		
EMAIL:		
IMPORTANCE: LOW ☐ MEDIUM ☐ HIGH ☐		CALLED ☐

DATE:	TIME:	MESSAGE:
NAME:		
COMPANY:		
PHONE:		
EMAIL:		
IMPORTANCE: LOW ☐ MEDIUM ☐ HIGH ☐		CALLED ☐

DATE:	TIME:	MESSAGE:
NAME:		
COMPANY:		
PHONE:		
EMAIL:		
IMPORTANCE: LOW ☐ MEDIUM ☐ HIGH ☐		CALLED ☐

DATE:	TIME:	MESSAGE:
NAME:		
COMPANY:		
PHONE:		
EMAIL:		
IMPORTANCE: LOW ☐ MEDIUM ☐ HIGH ☐		CALLED ☐

DATE:	TIME:	MESSAGE:
NAME:		
COMPANY:		
PHONE:		
EMAIL:		
IMPORTANCE: LOW ☐ MEDIUM ☐ HIGH ☐		CALLED ☐

DATE: **TIME:**	**MESSAGE:**
NAME:	
COMPANY:	
PHONE:	
EMAIL:	
IMPORTANCE: LOW ☐ **MEDIUM** ☐ **HIGH** ☐	**CALLED** ☐
DATE: **TIME:**	**MESSAGE:**
NAME:	
COMPANY:	
PHONE:	
EMAIL:	
IMPORTANCE: LOW ☐ **MEDIUM** ☐ **HIGH** ☐	**CALLED** ☐
DATE: **TIME:**	**MESSAGE:**
NAME:	
COMPANY:	
PHONE:	
EMAIL:	
IMPORTANCE: LOW ☐ **MEDIUM** ☐ **HIGH** ☐	**CALLED** ☐
DATE: **TIME:**	**MESSAGE:**
NAME:	
COMPANY:	
PHONE:	
EMAIL:	
IMPORTANCE: LOW ☐ **MEDIUM** ☐ **HIGH** ☐	**CALLED** ☐
DATE: **TIME:**	**MESSAGE:**
NAME:	
COMPANY:	
PHONE:	
EMAIL:	
IMPORTANCE: LOW ☐ **MEDIUM** ☐ **HIGH** ☐	**CALLED** ☐

DATE:	TIME:
NAME:	
COMPANY:	
PHONE:	
EMAIL:	
IMPORTANCE: LOW ☐ **MEDIUM** ☐ **HIGH** ☐	

MESSAGE:

CALLED ☐

DATE:	TIME:
NAME:	
COMPANY:	
PHONE:	
EMAIL:	
IMPORTANCE: LOW ☐ **MEDIUM** ☐ **HIGH** ☐	

MESSAGE:

CALLED ☐

DATE:	TIME:
NAME:	
COMPANY:	
PHONE:	
EMAIL:	
IMPORTANCE: LOW ☐ **MEDIUM** ☐ **HIGH** ☐	

MESSAGE:

CALLED ☐

DATE:	TIME:
NAME:	
COMPANY:	
PHONE:	
EMAIL:	
IMPORTANCE: LOW ☐ **MEDIUM** ☐ **HIGH** ☐	

MESSAGE:

CALLED ☐

DATE:	TIME:
NAME:	
COMPANY:	
PHONE:	
EMAIL:	
IMPORTANCE: LOW ☐ **MEDIUM** ☐ **HIGH** ☐	

MESSAGE:

CALLED ☐

DATE: **TIME:**	**MESSAGE:**
NAME:	
COMPANY:	
PHONE:	
EMAIL:	
IMPORTANCE: LOW ☐ **MEDIUM** ☐ **HIGH** ☐	**CALLED** ☐
DATE: **TIME:**	**MESSAGE:**
NAME:	
COMPANY:	
PHONE:	
EMAIL:	
IMPORTANCE: LOW ☐ **MEDIUM** ☐ **HIGH** ☐	**CALLED** ☐
DATE: **TIME:**	**MESSAGE:**
NAME:	
COMPANY:	
PHONE:	
EMAIL:	
IMPORTANCE: LOW ☐ **MEDIUM** ☐ **HIGH** ☐	**CALLED** ☐
DATE: **TIME:**	**MESSAGE:**
NAME:	
COMPANY:	
PHONE:	
EMAIL:	
IMPORTANCE: LOW ☐ **MEDIUM** ☐ **HIGH** ☐	**CALLED** ☐
DATE: **TIME:**	**MESSAGE:**
NAME:	
COMPANY:	
PHONE:	
EMAIL:	
IMPORTANCE: LOW ☐ **MEDIUM** ☐ **HIGH** ☐	**CALLED** ☐

DATE: **TIME:**	**MESSAGE:**
NAME:	
COMPANY:	
PHONE:	
EMAIL:	
IMPORTANCE: LOW ☐ **MEDIUM** ☐ **HIGH** ☐	**CALLED** ☐
DATE: **TIME:**	**MESSAGE:**
NAME:	
COMPANY:	
PHONE:	
EMAIL:	
IMPORTANCE: LOW ☐ **MEDIUM** ☐ **HIGH** ☐	**CALLED** ☐
DATE: **TIME:**	**MESSAGE:**
NAME:	
COMPANY:	
PHONE:	
EMAIL:	
IMPORTANCE: LOW ☐ **MEDIUM** ☐ **HIGH** ☐	**CALLED** ☐
DATE: **TIME:**	**MESSAGE:**
NAME:	
COMPANY:	
PHONE:	
EMAIL:	
IMPORTANCE: LOW ☐ **MEDIUM** ☐ **HIGH** ☐	**CALLED** ☐
DATE: **TIME:**	**MESSAGE:**
NAME:	
COMPANY:	
PHONE:	
EMAIL:	
IMPORTANCE: LOW ☐ **MEDIUM** ☐ **HIGH** ☐	**CALLED** ☐

DATE: TIME:	MESSAGE:
NAME:	
COMPANY:	
PHONE:	
EMAIL:	
IMPORTANCE: LOW ☐ MEDIUM ☐ HIGH ☐	CALLED ☐
DATE: TIME:	MESSAGE:
NAME:	
COMPANY:	
PHONE:	
EMAIL:	
IMPORTANCE: LOW ☐ MEDIUM ☐ HIGH ☐	CALLED ☐
DATE: TIME:	MESSAGE:
NAME:	
COMPANY:	
PHONE:	
EMAIL:	
IMPORTANCE: LOW ☐ MEDIUM ☐ HIGH ☐	CALLED ☐
DATE: TIME:	MESSAGE:
NAME:	
COMPANY:	
PHONE:	
EMAIL:	
IMPORTANCE: LOW ☐ MEDIUM ☐ HIGH ☐	CALLED ☐
DATE: TIME:	MESSAGE:
NAME:	
COMPANY:	
PHONE:	
EMAIL:	
IMPORTANCE: LOW ☐ MEDIUM ☐ HIGH ☐	CALLED ☐

DATE: **TIME:**	**MESSAGE:**
NAME:	
COMPANY:	
PHONE:	
EMAIL:	
IMPORTANCE: LOW ☐ **MEDIUM** ☐ **HIGH** ☐	**CALLED** ☐
DATE: **TIME:**	**MESSAGE:**
NAME:	
COMPANY:	
PHONE:	
EMAIL:	
IMPORTANCE: LOW ☐ **MEDIUM** ☐ **HIGH** ☐	**CALLED** ☐
DATE: **TIME:**	**MESSAGE:**
NAME:	
COMPANY:	
PHONE:	
EMAIL:	
IMPORTANCE: LOW ☐ **MEDIUM** ☐ **HIGH** ☐	**CALLED** ☐
DATE: **TIME:**	**MESSAGE:**
NAME:	
COMPANY:	
PHONE:	
EMAIL:	
IMPORTANCE: LOW ☐ **MEDIUM** ☐ **HIGH** ☐	**CALLED** ☐
DATE: **TIME:**	**MESSAGE:**
NAME:	
COMPANY:	
PHONE:	
EMAIL:	
IMPORTANCE: LOW ☐ **MEDIUM** ☐ **HIGH** ☐	**CALLED** ☐

DATE:　　　　　　**TIME:**	**MESSAGE:**
NAME:	
COMPANY:	
PHONE:	
EMAIL:	
IMPORTANCE: LOW ☐ **MEDIUM** ☐ **HIGH** ☐	**CALLED** ☐
DATE:　　　　　　**TIME:**	**MESSAGE:**
NAME:	
COMPANY:	
PHONE:	
EMAIL:	
IMPORTANCE: LOW ☐ **MEDIUM** ☐ **HIGH** ☐	**CALLED** ☐
DATE:　　　　　　**TIME:**	**MESSAGE:**
NAME:	
COMPANY:	
PHONE:	
EMAIL:	
IMPORTANCE: LOW ☐ **MEDIUM** ☐ **HIGH** ☐	**CALLED** ☐
DATE:　　　　　　**TIME:**	**MESSAGE:**
NAME:	
COMPANY:	
PHONE:	
EMAIL:	
IMPORTANCE: LOW ☐ **MEDIUM** ☐ **HIGH** ☐	**CALLED** ☐
DATE:　　　　　　**TIME:**	**MESSAGE:**
NAME:	
COMPANY:	
PHONE:	
EMAIL:	
IMPORTANCE: LOW ☐ **MEDIUM** ☐ **HIGH** ☐	**CALLED** ☐

	MESSAGE:
DATE: **TIME:**	
NAME:	
COMPANY:	
PHONE:	
EMAIL:	
IMPORTANCE: LOW ☐ **MEDIUM** ☐ **HIGH** ☐	**CALLED** ☐
DATE: **TIME:**	MESSAGE:
NAME:	
COMPANY:	
PHONE:	
EMAIL:	
IMPORTANCE: LOW ☐ **MEDIUM** ☐ **HIGH** ☐	**CALLED** ☐
DATE: **TIME:**	MESSAGE:
NAME:	
COMPANY:	
PHONE:	
EMAIL:	
IMPORTANCE: LOW ☐ **MEDIUM** ☐ **HIGH** ☐	**CALLED** ☐
DATE: **TIME:**	MESSAGE:
NAME:	
COMPANY:	
PHONE:	
EMAIL:	
IMPORTANCE: LOW ☐ **MEDIUM** ☐ **HIGH** ☐	**CALLED** ☐
DATE: **TIME:**	MESSAGE:
NAME:	
COMPANY:	
PHONE:	
EMAIL:	
IMPORTANCE: LOW ☐ **MEDIUM** ☐ **HIGH** ☐	**CALLED** ☐

DATE:	TIME:	MESSAGE:
NAME:		
COMPANY:		
PHONE:		
EMAIL:		
IMPORTANCE: LOW ☐ MEDIUM ☐ HIGH ☐		CALLED ☐

DATE:	TIME:	MESSAGE:
NAME:		
COMPANY:		
PHONE:		
EMAIL:		
IMPORTANCE: LOW ☐ MEDIUM ☐ HIGH ☐		CALLED ☐

DATE:	TIME:	MESSAGE:
NAME:		
COMPANY:		
PHONE:		
EMAIL:		
IMPORTANCE: LOW ☐ MEDIUM ☐ HIGH ☐		CALLED ☐

DATE:	TIME:	MESSAGE:
NAME:		
COMPANY:		
PHONE:		
EMAIL:		
IMPORTANCE: LOW ☐ MEDIUM ☐ HIGH ☐		CALLED ☐

DATE:	TIME:	MESSAGE:
NAME:		
COMPANY:		
PHONE:		
EMAIL:		
IMPORTANCE: LOW ☐ MEDIUM ☐ HIGH ☐		CALLED ☐

DATE: TIME:	MESSAGE:
NAME:	
COMPANY:	
PHONE:	
EMAIL:	
IMPORTANCE: LOW ▢ MEDIUM ▢ HIGH ▢	CALLED ▢
DATE: TIME:	MESSAGE:
NAME:	
COMPANY:	
PHONE:	
EMAIL:	
IMPORTANCE: LOW ▢ MEDIUM ▢ HIGH ▢	CALLED ▢
DATE: TIME:	MESSAGE:
NAME:	
COMPANY:	
PHONE:	
EMAIL:	
IMPORTANCE: LOW ▢ MEDIUM ▢ HIGH ▢	CALLED ▢
DATE: TIME:	MESSAGE:
NAME:	
COMPANY:	
PHONE:	
EMAIL:	
IMPORTANCE: LOW ▢ MEDIUM ▢ HIGH ▢	CALLED ▢
DATE: TIME:	MESSAGE:
NAME:	
COMPANY:	
PHONE:	
EMAIL:	
IMPORTANCE: LOW ▢ MEDIUM ▢ HIGH ▢	CALLED ▢

DATE: **TIME:**	**MESSAGE:**
NAME:	
COMPANY:	
PHONE:	
EMAIL:	
IMPORTANCE: LOW ☐ **MEDIUM** ☐ **HIGH** ☐	**CALLED** ☐
DATE: **TIME:**	**MESSAGE:**
NAME:	
COMPANY:	
PHONE:	
EMAIL:	
IMPORTANCE: LOW ☐ **MEDIUM** ☐ **HIGH** ☐	**CALLED** ☐
DATE: **TIME:**	**MESSAGE:**
NAME:	
COMPANY:	
PHONE:	
EMAIL:	
IMPORTANCE: LOW ☐ **MEDIUM** ☐ **HIGH** ☐	**CALLED** ☐
DATE: **TIME:**	**MESSAGE:**
NAME:	
COMPANY:	
PHONE:	
EMAIL:	
IMPORTANCE: LOW ☐ **MEDIUM** ☐ **HIGH** ☐	**CALLED** ☐
DATE: **TIME:**	**MESSAGE:**
NAME:	
COMPANY:	
PHONE:	
EMAIL:	
IMPORTANCE: LOW ☐ **MEDIUM** ☐ **HIGH** ☐	**CALLED** ☐

DATE:	TIME:	MESSAGE:
NAME:		
COMPANY:		
PHONE:		
EMAIL:		
IMPORTANCE: LOW ☐ MEDIUM ☐ HIGH ☐		CALLED ☐

DATE:	TIME:	MESSAGE:
NAME:		
COMPANY:		
PHONE:		
EMAIL:		
IMPORTANCE: LOW ☐ MEDIUM ☐ HIGH ☐		CALLED ☐

DATE:	TIME:	MESSAGE:
NAME:		
COMPANY:		
PHONE:		
EMAIL:		
IMPORTANCE: LOW ☐ MEDIUM ☐ HIGH ☐		CALLED ☐

DATE:	TIME:	MESSAGE:
NAME:		
COMPANY:		
PHONE:		
EMAIL:		
IMPORTANCE: LOW ☐ MEDIUM ☐ HIGH ☐		CALLED ☐

DATE:	TIME:	MESSAGE:
NAME:		
COMPANY:		
PHONE:		
EMAIL:		
IMPORTANCE: LOW ☐ MEDIUM ☐ HIGH ☐		CALLED ☐

DATE: **TIME:**	**MESSAGE:**
NAME:	
COMPANY:	
PHONE:	
EMAIL:	
IMPORTANCE: LOW ☐ **MEDIUM** ☐ **HIGH** ☐	**CALLED** ☐
DATE: **TIME:**	**MESSAGE:**
NAME:	
COMPANY:	
PHONE:	
EMAIL:	
IMPORTANCE: LOW ☐ **MEDIUM** ☐ **HIGH** ☐	**CALLED** ☐
DATE: **TIME:**	**MESSAGE:**
NAME:	
COMPANY:	
PHONE:	
EMAIL:	
IMPORTANCE: LOW ☐ **MEDIUM** ☐ **HIGH** ☐	**CALLED** ☐
DATE: **TIME:**	**MESSAGE:**
NAME:	
COMPANY:	
PHONE:	
EMAIL:	
IMPORTANCE: LOW ☐ **MEDIUM** ☐ **HIGH** ☐	**CALLED** ☐
DATE: **TIME:**	**MESSAGE:**
NAME:	
COMPANY:	
PHONE:	
EMAIL:	
IMPORTANCE: LOW ☐ **MEDIUM** ☐ **HIGH** ☐	**CALLED** ☐

DATE: **TIME:**	**MESSAGE:**
NAME:	
COMPANY:	
PHONE:	
EMAIL:	
IMPORTANCE: LOW ☐ MEDIUM ☐ HIGH ☐	**CALLED** ☐
DATE: **TIME:**	**MESSAGE:**
NAME:	
COMPANY:	
PHONE:	
EMAIL:	
IMPORTANCE: LOW ☐ MEDIUM ☐ HIGH ☐	**CALLED** ☐
DATE: **TIME:**	**MESSAGE:**
NAME:	
COMPANY:	
PHONE:	
EMAIL:	
IMPORTANCE: LOW ☐ MEDIUM ☐ HIGH ☐	**CALLED** ☐
DATE: **TIME:**	**MESSAGE:**
NAME:	
COMPANY:	
PHONE:	
EMAIL:	
IMPORTANCE: LOW ☐ MEDIUM ☐ HIGH ☐	**CALLED** ☐
DATE: **TIME:**	**MESSAGE:**
NAME:	
COMPANY:	
PHONE:	
EMAIL:	
IMPORTANCE: LOW ☐ MEDIUM ☐ HIGH ☐	**CALLED** ☐

DATE:	TIME:	MESSAGE:
NAME:		
COMPANY:		
PHONE:		
EMAIL:		
IMPORTANCE: LOW ☐ MEDIUM ☐ HIGH ☐		CALLED ☐

DATE:	TIME:	MESSAGE:
NAME:		
COMPANY:		
PHONE:		
EMAIL:		
IMPORTANCE: LOW ☐ MEDIUM ☐ HIGH ☐		CALLED ☐

DATE:	TIME:	MESSAGE:
NAME:		
COMPANY:		
PHONE:		
EMAIL:		
IMPORTANCE: LOW ☐ MEDIUM ☐ HIGH ☐		CALLED ☐

DATE:	TIME:	MESSAGE:
NAME:		
COMPANY:		
PHONE:		
EMAIL:		
IMPORTANCE: LOW ☐ MEDIUM ☐ HIGH ☐		CALLED ☐

DATE:	TIME:	MESSAGE:
NAME:		
COMPANY:		
PHONE:		
EMAIL:		
IMPORTANCE: LOW ☐ MEDIUM ☐ HIGH ☐		CALLED ☐

DATE: **TIME:**	**MESSAGE:**
NAME:	
COMPANY:	
PHONE:	
EMAIL:	
IMPORTANCE: LOW ☐ **MEDIUM** ☐ **HIGH** ☐	**CALLED** ☐
DATE: **TIME:**	**MESSAGE:**
NAME:	
COMPANY:	
PHONE:	
EMAIL:	
IMPORTANCE: LOW ☐ **MEDIUM** ☐ **HIGH** ☐	**CALLED** ☐
DATE: **TIME:**	**MESSAGE:**
NAME:	
COMPANY:	
PHONE:	
EMAIL:	
IMPORTANCE: LOW ☐ **MEDIUM** ☐ **HIGH** ☐	**CALLED** ☐
DATE: **TIME:**	**MESSAGE:**
NAME:	
COMPANY:	
PHONE:	
EMAIL:	
IMPORTANCE: LOW ☐ **MEDIUM** ☐ **HIGH** ☐	**CALLED** ☐
DATE: **TIME:**	**MESSAGE:**
NAME:	
COMPANY:	
PHONE:	
EMAIL:	
IMPORTANCE: LOW ☐ **MEDIUM** ☐ **HIGH** ☐	**CALLED** ☐

DATE:	TIME:	MESSAGE:
NAME:		
COMPANY:		
PHONE:		
EMAIL:		
IMPORTANCE: LOW ☐ MEDIUM ☐ HIGH ☐		CALLED ☐

DATE:	TIME:	MESSAGE:
NAME:		
COMPANY:		
PHONE:		
EMAIL:		
IMPORTANCE: LOW ☐ MEDIUM ☐ HIGH ☐		CALLED ☐

DATE:	TIME:	MESSAGE:
NAME:		
COMPANY:		
PHONE:		
EMAIL:		
IMPORTANCE: LOW ☐ MEDIUM ☐ HIGH ☐		CALLED ☐

DATE:	TIME:	MESSAGE:
NAME:		
COMPANY:		
PHONE:		
EMAIL:		
IMPORTANCE: LOW ☐ MEDIUM ☐ HIGH ☐		CALLED ☐

DATE:	TIME:	MESSAGE:
NAME:		
COMPANY:		
PHONE:		
EMAIL:		
IMPORTANCE: LOW ☐ MEDIUM ☐ HIGH ☐		CALLED ☐

DATE: TIME:	**MESSAGE:**
NAME:	
COMPANY:	
PHONE:	
EMAIL:	
IMPORTANCE: LOW ☐ **MEDIUM** ☐ **HIGH** ☐	**CALLED** ☐
DATE: TIME:	**MESSAGE:**
NAME:	
COMPANY:	
PHONE:	
EMAIL:	
IMPORTANCE: LOW ☐ **MEDIUM** ☐ **HIGH** ☐	**CALLED** ☐
DATE: TIME:	**MESSAGE:**
NAME:	
COMPANY:	
PHONE:	
EMAIL:	
IMPORTANCE: LOW ☐ **MEDIUM** ☐ **HIGH** ☐	**CALLED** ☐
DATE: TIME:	**MESSAGE:**
NAME:	
COMPANY:	
PHONE:	
EMAIL:	
IMPORTANCE: LOW ☐ **MEDIUM** ☐ **HIGH** ☐	**CALLED** ☐
DATE: TIME:	**MESSAGE:**
NAME:	
COMPANY:	
PHONE:	
EMAIL:	
IMPORTANCE: LOW ☐ **MEDIUM** ☐ **HIGH** ☐	**CALLED** ☐

DATE:	TIME:	MESSAGE:
NAME:		
COMPANY:		
PHONE:		
EMAIL:		
IMPORTANCE: LOW ☐ MEDIUM ☐ HIGH ☐		**CALLED** ☐

DATE:	TIME:	MESSAGE:
NAME:		
COMPANY:		
PHONE:		
EMAIL:		
IMPORTANCE: LOW ☐ MEDIUM ☐ HIGH ☐		**CALLED** ☐

DATE:	TIME:	MESSAGE:
NAME:		
COMPANY:		
PHONE:		
EMAIL:		
IMPORTANCE: LOW ☐ MEDIUM ☐ HIGH ☐		**CALLED** ☐

DATE:	TIME:	MESSAGE:
NAME:		
COMPANY:		
PHONE:		
EMAIL:		
IMPORTANCE: LOW ☐ MEDIUM ☐ HIGH ☐		**CALLED** ☐

DATE:	TIME:	MESSAGE:
NAME:		
COMPANY:		
PHONE:		
EMAIL:		
IMPORTANCE: LOW ☐ MEDIUM ☐ HIGH ☐		**CALLED** ☐

DATE: TIME:	MESSAGE:
NAME:	
COMPANY:	
PHONE:	
EMAIL:	
IMPORTANCE: LOW ☐ MEDIUM ☐ HIGH ☐	CALLED ☐
DATE: TIME:	MESSAGE:
NAME:	
COMPANY:	
PHONE:	
EMAIL:	
IMPORTANCE: LOW ☐ MEDIUM ☐ HIGH ☐	CALLED ☐
DATE: TIME:	MESSAGE:
NAME:	
COMPANY:	
PHONE:	
EMAIL:	
IMPORTANCE: LOW ☐ MEDIUM ☐ HIGH ☐	CALLED ☐
DATE: TIME:	MESSAGE:
NAME:	
COMPANY:	
PHONE:	
EMAIL:	
IMPORTANCE: LOW ☐ MEDIUM ☐ HIGH ☐	CALLED ☐
DATE: TIME:	MESSAGE:
NAME:	
COMPANY:	
PHONE:	
EMAIL:	
IMPORTANCE: LOW ☐ MEDIUM ☐ HIGH ☐	CALLED ☐

DATE: TIME:	MESSAGE:
NAME:	
COMPANY:	
PHONE:	
EMAIL:	
IMPORTANCE: LOW ☐ MEDIUM ☐ HIGH ☐	CALLED ☐
DATE: TIME:	MESSAGE:
NAME:	
COMPANY:	
PHONE:	
EMAIL:	
IMPORTANCE: LOW ☐ MEDIUM ☐ HIGH ☐	CALLED ☐
DATE: TIME:	MESSAGE:
NAME:	
COMPANY:	
PHONE:	
EMAIL:	
IMPORTANCE: LOW ☐ MEDIUM ☐ HIGH ☐	CALLED ☐
DATE: TIME:	MESSAGE:
NAME:	
COMPANY:	
PHONE:	
EMAIL:	
IMPORTANCE: LOW ☐ MEDIUM ☐ HIGH ☐	CALLED ☐
DATE: TIME:	MESSAGE:
NAME:	
COMPANY:	
PHONE:	
EMAIL:	
IMPORTANCE: LOW ☐ MEDIUM ☐ HIGH ☐	CALLED ☐

DATE:	TIME:	MESSAGE:
NAME:		
COMPANY:		
PHONE:		
EMAIL:		
IMPORTANCE: LOW ☐ MEDIUM ☐ HIGH ☐		CALLED ☐

DATE:	TIME:	MESSAGE:
NAME:		
COMPANY:		
PHONE:		
EMAIL:		
IMPORTANCE: LOW ☐ MEDIUM ☐ HIGH ☐		CALLED ☐

DATE:	TIME:	MESSAGE:
NAME:		
COMPANY:		
PHONE:		
EMAIL:		
IMPORTANCE: LOW ☐ MEDIUM ☐ HIGH ☐		CALLED ☐

DATE:	TIME:	MESSAGE:
NAME:		
COMPANY:		
PHONE:		
EMAIL:		
IMPORTANCE: LOW ☐ MEDIUM ☐ HIGH ☐		CALLED ☐

DATE:	TIME:	MESSAGE:
NAME:		
COMPANY:		
PHONE:		
EMAIL:		
IMPORTANCE: LOW ☐ MEDIUM ☐ HIGH ☐		CALLED ☐

DATE: **TIME:**	**MESSAGE:**
NAME:	
COMPANY:	
PHONE:	
EMAIL:	
IMPORTANCE: LOW ☐ **MEDIUM** ☐ **HIGH** ☐	**CALLED** ☐
DATE: **TIME:**	**MESSAGE:**
NAME:	
COMPANY:	
PHONE:	
EMAIL:	
IMPORTANCE: LOW ☐ **MEDIUM** ☐ **HIGH** ☐	**CALLED** ☐
DATE: **TIME:**	**MESSAGE:**
NAME:	
COMPANY:	
PHONE:	
EMAIL:	
IMPORTANCE: LOW ☐ **MEDIUM** ☐ **HIGH** ☐	**CALLED** ☐
DATE: **TIME:**	**MESSAGE:**
NAME:	
COMPANY:	
PHONE:	
EMAIL:	
IMPORTANCE: LOW ☐ **MEDIUM** ☐ **HIGH** ☐	**CALLED** ☐
DATE: **TIME:**	**MESSAGE:**
NAME:	
COMPANY:	
PHONE:	
EMAIL:	
IMPORTANCE: LOW ☐ **MEDIUM** ☐ **HIGH** ☐	**CALLED** ☐

DATE:	TIME:	MESSAGE:
NAME:		
COMPANY:		
PHONE:		
EMAIL:		
IMPORTANCE: LOW ☐ MEDIUM ☐ HIGH ☐		CALLED ☐

DATE:	TIME:	MESSAGE:
NAME:		
COMPANY:		
PHONE:		
EMAIL:		
IMPORTANCE: LOW ☐ MEDIUM ☐ HIGH ☐		CALLED ☐

DATE:	TIME:	MESSAGE:
NAME:		
COMPANY:		
PHONE:		
EMAIL:		
IMPORTANCE: LOW ☐ MEDIUM ☐ HIGH ☐		CALLED ☐

DATE:	TIME:	MESSAGE:
NAME:		
COMPANY:		
PHONE:		
EMAIL:		
IMPORTANCE: LOW ☐ MEDIUM ☐ HIGH ☐		CALLED ☐

DATE:	TIME:	MESSAGE:
NAME:		
COMPANY:		
PHONE:		
EMAIL:		
IMPORTANCE: LOW ☐ MEDIUM ☐ HIGH ☐		CALLED ☐

DATE:	TIME:	MESSAGE:
NAME:		
COMPANY:		
PHONE:		
EMAIL:		
IMPORTANCE: LOW ☐ MEDIUM ☐ HIGH ☐		CALLED ☐

DATE:	TIME:	MESSAGE:
NAME:		
COMPANY:		
PHONE:		
EMAIL:		
IMPORTANCE: LOW ☐ MEDIUM ☐ HIGH ☐		CALLED ☐

DATE:	TIME:	MESSAGE:
NAME:		
COMPANY:		
PHONE:		
EMAIL:		
IMPORTANCE: LOW ☐ MEDIUM ☐ HIGH ☐		CALLED ☐

DATE:	TIME:	MESSAGE:
NAME:		
COMPANY:		
PHONE:		
EMAIL:		
IMPORTANCE: LOW ☐ MEDIUM ☐ HIGH ☐		CALLED ☐

DATE:	TIME:	MESSAGE:
NAME:		
COMPANY:		
PHONE:		
EMAIL:		
IMPORTANCE: LOW ☐ MEDIUM ☐ HIGH ☐		CALLED ☐

DATE:	TIME:	MESSAGE:
NAME:		
COMPANY:		
PHONE:		
EMAIL:		
IMPORTANCE: LOW ☐ MEDIUM ☐ HIGH ☐		CALLED ☐

DATE:	TIME:	MESSAGE:
NAME:		
COMPANY:		
PHONE:		
EMAIL:		
IMPORTANCE: LOW ☐ MEDIUM ☐ HIGH ☐		CALLED ☐

DATE:	TIME:	MESSAGE:
NAME:		
COMPANY:		
PHONE:		
EMAIL:		
IMPORTANCE: LOW ☐ MEDIUM ☐ HIGH ☐		CALLED ☐

DATE:	TIME:	MESSAGE:
NAME:		
COMPANY:		
PHONE:		
EMAIL:		
IMPORTANCE: LOW ☐ MEDIUM ☐ HIGH ☐		CALLED ☐

DATE:	TIME:	MESSAGE:
NAME:		
COMPANY:		
PHONE:		
EMAIL:		
IMPORTANCE: LOW ☐ MEDIUM ☐ HIGH ☐		CALLED ☐

DATE: **TIME:**	**MESSAGE:**
NAME:	
COMPANY:	
PHONE:	
EMAIL:	
IMPORTANCE: LOW ☐ **MEDIUM** ☐ **HIGH** ☐	**CALLED** ☐
DATE: **TIME:**	**MESSAGE:**
NAME:	
COMPANY:	
PHONE:	
EMAIL:	
IMPORTANCE: LOW ☐ **MEDIUM** ☐ **HIGH** ☐	**CALLED** ☐
DATE: **TIME:**	**MESSAGE:**
NAME:	
COMPANY:	
PHONE:	
EMAIL:	
IMPORTANCE: LOW ☐ **MEDIUM** ☐ **HIGH** ☐	**CALLED** ☐
DATE: **TIME:**	**MESSAGE:**
NAME:	
COMPANY:	
PHONE:	
EMAIL:	
IMPORTANCE: LOW ☐ **MEDIUM** ☐ **HIGH** ☐	**CALLED** ☐
DATE: **TIME:**	**MESSAGE:**
NAME:	
COMPANY:	
PHONE:	
EMAIL:	
IMPORTANCE: LOW ☐ **MEDIUM** ☐ **HIGH** ☐	**CALLED** ☐

DATE: TIME:	MESSAGE:
NAME:	
COMPANY:	
PHONE:	
EMAIL:	
IMPORTANCE: LOW ☐ MEDIUM ☐ HIGH ☐	CALLED ☐
DATE: TIME:	MESSAGE:
NAME:	
COMPANY:	
PHONE:	
EMAIL:	
IMPORTANCE: LOW ☐ MEDIUM ☐ HIGH ☐	CALLED ☐
DATE: TIME:	MESSAGE:
NAME:	
COMPANY:	
PHONE:	
EMAIL:	
IMPORTANCE: LOW ☐ MEDIUM ☐ HIGH ☐	CALLED ☐
DATE: TIME:	MESSAGE:
NAME:	
COMPANY:	
PHONE:	
EMAIL:	
IMPORTANCE: LOW ☐ MEDIUM ☐ HIGH ☐	CALLED ☐
DATE: TIME:	MESSAGE:
NAME:	
COMPANY:	
PHONE:	
EMAIL:	
IMPORTANCE: LOW ☐ MEDIUM ☐ HIGH ☐	CALLED ☐

DATE:	TIME:	MESSAGE:
NAME:		
COMPANY:		
PHONE:		
EMAIL:		
IMPORTANCE: LOW ☐ MEDIUM ☐ HIGH ☐		CALLED ☐

DATE:	TIME:	MESSAGE:
NAME:		
COMPANY:		
PHONE:		
EMAIL:		
IMPORTANCE: LOW ☐ MEDIUM ☐ HIGH ☐		CALLED ☐

DATE:	TIME:	MESSAGE:
NAME:		
COMPANY:		
PHONE:		
EMAIL:		
IMPORTANCE: LOW ☐ MEDIUM ☐ HIGH ☐		CALLED ☐

DATE:	TIME:	MESSAGE:
NAME:		
COMPANY:		
PHONE:		
EMAIL:		
IMPORTANCE: LOW ☐ MEDIUM ☐ HIGH ☐		CALLED ☐

DATE:	TIME:	MESSAGE:
NAME:		
COMPANY:		
PHONE:		
EMAIL:		
IMPORTANCE: LOW ☐ MEDIUM ☐ HIGH ☐		CALLED ☐

DATE: **TIME:**	**MESSAGE:**
NAME:	
COMPANY:	
PHONE:	
EMAIL:	
IMPORTANCE: LOW ☐ **MEDIUM** ☐ **HIGH** ☐	**CALLED** ☐
DATE: **TIME:**	**MESSAGE:**
NAME:	
COMPANY:	
PHONE:	
EMAIL:	
IMPORTANCE: LOW ☐ **MEDIUM** ☐ **HIGH** ☐	**CALLED** ☐
DATE: **TIME:**	**MESSAGE:**
NAME:	
COMPANY:	
PHONE:	
EMAIL:	
IMPORTANCE: LOW ☐ **MEDIUM** ☐ **HIGH** ☐	**CALLED** ☐
DATE: **TIME:**	**MESSAGE:**
NAME:	
COMPANY:	
PHONE:	
EMAIL:	
IMPORTANCE: LOW ☐ **MEDIUM** ☐ **HIGH** ☐	**CALLED** ☐
DATE: **TIME:**	**MESSAGE:**
NAME:	
COMPANY:	
PHONE:	
EMAIL:	
IMPORTANCE: LOW ☐ **MEDIUM** ☐ **HIGH** ☐	**CALLED** ☐

DATE:	TIME:	MESSAGE:
NAME:		
COMPANY:		
PHONE:		
EMAIL:		
IMPORTANCE: LOW ▢ MEDIUM ▢ HIGH ▢		CALLED ▢

DATE:	TIME:	MESSAGE:
NAME:		
COMPANY:		
PHONE:		
EMAIL:		
IMPORTANCE: LOW ▢ MEDIUM ▢ HIGH ▢		CALLED ▢

DATE:	TIME:	MESSAGE:
NAME:		
COMPANY:		
PHONE:		
EMAIL:		
IMPORTANCE: LOW ▢ MEDIUM ▢ HIGH ▢		CALLED ▢

DATE:	TIME:	MESSAGE:
NAME:		
COMPANY:		
PHONE:		
EMAIL:		
IMPORTANCE: LOW ▢ MEDIUM ▢ HIGH ▢		CALLED ▢

DATE:	TIME:	MESSAGE:
NAME:		
COMPANY:		
PHONE:		
EMAIL:		
IMPORTANCE: LOW ▢ MEDIUM ▢ HIGH ▢		CALLED ▢

DATE: **TIME:**	**MESSAGE:**
NAME:	
COMPANY:	
PHONE:	
EMAIL:	
IMPORTANCE: LOW ☐ MEDIUM ☐ HIGH ☐	**CALLED** ☐
DATE: **TIME:**	**MESSAGE:**
NAME:	
COMPANY:	
PHONE:	
EMAIL:	
IMPORTANCE: LOW ☐ MEDIUM ☐ HIGH ☐	**CALLED** ☐
DATE: **TIME:**	**MESSAGE:**
NAME:	
COMPANY:	
PHONE:	
EMAIL:	
IMPORTANCE: LOW ☐ MEDIUM ☐ HIGH ☐	**CALLED** ☐
DATE: **TIME:**	**MESSAGE:**
NAME:	
COMPANY:	
PHONE:	
EMAIL:	
IMPORTANCE: LOW ☐ MEDIUM ☐ HIGH ☐	**CALLED** ☐
DATE: **TIME:**	**MESSAGE:**
NAME:	
COMPANY:	
PHONE:	
EMAIL:	
IMPORTANCE: LOW ☐ MEDIUM ☐ HIGH ☐	**CALLED** ☐

DATE:	TIME:	MESSAGE:
NAME:		
COMPANY:		
PHONE:		
EMAIL:		
IMPORTANCE: LOW ☐ MEDIUM ☐ HIGH ☐		CALLED ☐
DATE:	TIME:	MESSAGE:
NAME:		
COMPANY:		
PHONE:		
EMAIL:		
IMPORTANCE: LOW ☐ MEDIUM ☐ HIGH ☐		CALLED ☐
DATE:	TIME:	MESSAGE:
NAME:		
COMPANY:		
PHONE:		
EMAIL:		
IMPORTANCE: LOW ☐ MEDIUM ☐ HIGH ☐		CALLED ☐
DATE:	TIME:	MESSAGE:
NAME:		
COMPANY:		
PHONE:		
EMAIL:		
IMPORTANCE: LOW ☐ MEDIUM ☐ HIGH ☐		CALLED ☐
DATE:	TIME:	MESSAGE:
NAME:		
COMPANY:		
PHONE:		
EMAIL:		
IMPORTANCE: LOW ☐ MEDIUM ☐ HIGH ☐		CALLED ☐

DATE: TIME:	MESSAGE:
NAME:	
COMPANY:	
PHONE:	
EMAIL:	
IMPORTANCE: LOW ☐ MEDIUM ☐ HIGH ☐	CALLED ☐
DATE: TIME:	MESSAGE:
NAME:	
COMPANY:	
PHONE:	
EMAIL:	
IMPORTANCE: LOW ☐ MEDIUM ☐ HIGH ☐	CALLED ☐
DATE: TIME:	MESSAGE:
NAME:	
COMPANY:	
PHONE:	
EMAIL:	
IMPORTANCE: LOW ☐ MEDIUM ☐ HIGH ☐	CALLED ☐
DATE: TIME:	MESSAGE:
NAME:	
COMPANY:	
PHONE:	
EMAIL:	
IMPORTANCE: LOW ☐ MEDIUM ☐ HIGH ☐	CALLED ☐
DATE: TIME:	MESSAGE:
NAME:	
COMPANY:	
PHONE:	
EMAIL:	
IMPORTANCE: LOW ☐ MEDIUM ☐ HIGH ☐	CALLED ☐

DATE:　　　　**TIME:**	**MESSAGE:**
NAME:	
COMPANY:	
PHONE:	
EMAIL:	
IMPORTANCE: LOW ☐ **MEDIUM** ☐ **HIGH** ☐	**CALLED** ☐
DATE:　　　　**TIME:**	**MESSAGE:**
NAME:	
COMPANY:	
PHONE:	
EMAIL:	
IMPORTANCE: LOW ☐ **MEDIUM** ☐ **HIGH** ☐	**CALLED** ☐
DATE:　　　　**TIME:**	**MESSAGE:**
NAME:	
COMPANY:	
PHONE:	
EMAIL:	
IMPORTANCE: LOW ☐ **MEDIUM** ☐ **HIGH** ☐	**CALLED** ☐
DATE:　　　　**TIME:**	**MESSAGE:**
NAME:	
COMPANY:	
PHONE:	
EMAIL:	
IMPORTANCE: LOW ☐ **MEDIUM** ☐ **HIGH** ☐	**CALLED** ☐
DATE:　　　　**TIME:**	**MESSAGE:**
NAME:	
COMPANY:	
PHONE:	
EMAIL:	
IMPORTANCE: LOW ☐ **MEDIUM** ☐ **HIGH** ☐	**CALLED** ☐

DATE: **TIME:**	**MESSAGE:**
NAME:	
COMPANY:	
PHONE:	
EMAIL:	
IMPORTANCE: LOW ☐ **MEDIUM** ☐ **HIGH** ☐	**CALLED** ☐
DATE: **TIME:**	**MESSAGE:**
NAME:	
COMPANY:	
PHONE:	
EMAIL:	
IMPORTANCE: LOW ☐ **MEDIUM** ☐ **HIGH** ☐	**CALLED** ☐
DATE: **TIME:**	**MESSAGE:**
NAME:	
COMPANY:	
PHONE:	
EMAIL:	
IMPORTANCE: LOW ☐ **MEDIUM** ☐ **HIGH** ☐	**CALLED** ☐
DATE: **TIME:**	**MESSAGE:**
NAME:	
COMPANY:	
PHONE:	
EMAIL:	
IMPORTANCE: LOW ☐ **MEDIUM** ☐ **HIGH** ☐	**CALLED** ☐
DATE: **TIME:**	**MESSAGE:**
NAME:	
COMPANY:	
PHONE:	
EMAIL:	
IMPORTANCE: LOW ☐ **MEDIUM** ☐ **HIGH** ☐	**CALLED** ☐

DATE:	TIME:	MESSAGE:
NAME:		
COMPANY:		
PHONE:		
EMAIL:		
IMPORTANCE: LOW ☐ MEDIUM ☐ HIGH ☐		CALLED ☐

DATE:	TIME:	MESSAGE:
NAME:		
COMPANY:		
PHONE:		
EMAIL:		
IMPORTANCE: LOW ☐ MEDIUM ☐ HIGH ☐		CALLED ☐

DATE:	TIME:	MESSAGE:
NAME:		
COMPANY:		
PHONE:		
EMAIL:		
IMPORTANCE: LOW ☐ MEDIUM ☐ HIGH ☐		CALLED ☐

DATE:	TIME:	MESSAGE:
NAME:		
COMPANY:		
PHONE:		
EMAIL:		
IMPORTANCE: LOW ☐ MEDIUM ☐ HIGH ☐		CALLED ☐

DATE:	TIME:	MESSAGE:
NAME:		
COMPANY:		
PHONE:		
EMAIL:		
IMPORTANCE: LOW ☐ MEDIUM ☐ HIGH ☐		CALLED ☐

DATE: **TIME:**	**MESSAGE:**
NAME:	
COMPANY:	
PHONE:	
EMAIL:	
IMPORTANCE: LOW ☐ **MEDIUM** ☐ **HIGH** ☐	**CALLED** ☐
DATE: **TIME:**	**MESSAGE:**
NAME:	
COMPANY:	
PHONE:	
EMAIL:	
IMPORTANCE: LOW ☐ **MEDIUM** ☐ **HIGH** ☐	**CALLED** ☐
DATE: **TIME:**	**MESSAGE:**
NAME:	
COMPANY:	
PHONE:	
EMAIL:	
IMPORTANCE: LOW ☐ **MEDIUM** ☐ **HIGH** ☐	**CALLED** ☐
DATE: **TIME:**	**MESSAGE:**
NAME:	
COMPANY:	
PHONE:	
EMAIL:	
IMPORTANCE: LOW ☐ **MEDIUM** ☐ **HIGH** ☐	**CALLED** ☐
DATE: **TIME:**	**MESSAGE:**
NAME:	
COMPANY:	
PHONE:	
EMAIL:	
IMPORTANCE: LOW ☐ **MEDIUM** ☐ **HIGH** ☐	**CALLED** ☐

DATE: TIME:	MESSAGE:
NAME:	
COMPANY:	
PHONE:	
EMAIL:	
IMPORTANCE: LOW ☐ MEDIUM ☐ HIGH ☐	CALLED ☐
DATE: TIME:	MESSAGE:
NAME:	
COMPANY:	
PHONE:	
EMAIL:	
IMPORTANCE: LOW ☐ MEDIUM ☐ HIGH ☐	CALLED ☐
DATE: TIME:	MESSAGE:
NAME:	
COMPANY:	
PHONE:	
EMAIL:	
IMPORTANCE: LOW ☐ MEDIUM ☐ HIGH ☐	CALLED ☐
DATE: TIME:	MESSAGE:
NAME:	
COMPANY:	
PHONE:	
EMAIL:	
IMPORTANCE: LOW ☐ MEDIUM ☐ HIGH ☐	CALLED ☐
DATE: TIME:	MESSAGE:
NAME:	
COMPANY:	
PHONE:	
EMAIL:	
IMPORTANCE: LOW ☐ MEDIUM ☐ HIGH ☐	CALLED ☐

DATE: **TIME:**	**MESSAGE:**
NAME:	
COMPANY:	
PHONE:	
EMAIL:	
IMPORTANCE: LOW ☐ **MEDIUM** ☐ **HIGH** ☐	**CALLED** ☐
DATE: **TIME:**	**MESSAGE:**
NAME:	
COMPANY:	
PHONE:	
EMAIL:	
IMPORTANCE: LOW ☐ **MEDIUM** ☐ **HIGH** ☐	**CALLED** ☐
DATE: **TIME:**	**MESSAGE:**
NAME:	
COMPANY:	
PHONE:	
EMAIL:	
IMPORTANCE: LOW ☐ **MEDIUM** ☐ **HIGH** ☐	**CALLED** ☐
DATE: **TIME:**	**MESSAGE:**
NAME:	
COMPANY:	
PHONE:	
EMAIL:	
IMPORTANCE: LOW ☐ **MEDIUM** ☐ **HIGH** ☐	**CALLED** ☐
DATE: **TIME:**	**MESSAGE:**
NAME:	
COMPANY:	
PHONE:	
EMAIL:	
IMPORTANCE: LOW ☐ **MEDIUM** ☐ **HIGH** ☐	**CALLED** ☐

DATE: **TIME:**	**MESSAGE:**
NAME:	
COMPANY:	
PHONE:	
EMAIL:	
IMPORTANCE: LOW ▢ **MEDIUM** ▢ **HIGH** ▢	**CALLED** ▢
DATE: **TIME:**	**MESSAGE:**
NAME:	
COMPANY:	
PHONE:	
EMAIL:	
IMPORTANCE: LOW ▢ **MEDIUM** ▢ **HIGH** ▢	**CALLED** ▢
DATE: **TIME:**	**MESSAGE:**
NAME:	
COMPANY:	
PHONE:	
EMAIL:	
IMPORTANCE: LOW ▢ **MEDIUM** ▢ **HIGH** ▢	**CALLED** ▢
DATE: **TIME:**	**MESSAGE:**
NAME:	
COMPANY:	
PHONE:	
EMAIL:	
IMPORTANCE: LOW ▢ **MEDIUM** ▢ **HIGH** ▢	**CALLED** ▢
DATE: **TIME:**	**MESSAGE:**
NAME:	
COMPANY:	
PHONE:	
EMAIL:	
IMPORTANCE: LOW ▢ **MEDIUM** ▢ **HIGH** ▢	**CALLED** ▢

	MESSAGE:
DATE: **TIME:**	
NAME:	
COMPANY:	
PHONE:	
EMAIL:	
IMPORTANCE: LOW ☐ **MEDIUM** ☐ **HIGH** ☐	**CALLED** ☐

	MESSAGE:
DATE: **TIME:**	
NAME:	
COMPANY:	
PHONE:	
EMAIL:	
IMPORTANCE: LOW ☐ **MEDIUM** ☐ **HIGH** ☐	**CALLED** ☐

	MESSAGE:
DATE: **TIME:**	
NAME:	
COMPANY:	
PHONE:	
EMAIL:	
IMPORTANCE: LOW ☐ **MEDIUM** ☐ **HIGH** ☐	**CALLED** ☐

	MESSAGE:
DATE: **TIME:**	
NAME:	
COMPANY:	
PHONE:	
EMAIL:	
IMPORTANCE: LOW ☐ **MEDIUM** ☐ **HIGH** ☐	**CALLED** ☐

	MESSAGE:
DATE: **TIME:**	
NAME:	
COMPANY:	
PHONE:	
EMAIL:	
IMPORTANCE: LOW ☐ **MEDIUM** ☐ **HIGH** ☐	**CALLED** ☐

	MESSAGE:
DATE: **TIME:**	
NAME:	
COMPANY:	
PHONE:	
EMAIL:	
IMPORTANCE: LOW ☐ **MEDIUM** ☐ **HIGH** ☐	**CALLED** ☐
DATE: **TIME:**	**MESSAGE:**
NAME:	
COMPANY:	
PHONE:	
EMAIL:	
IMPORTANCE: LOW ☐ **MEDIUM** ☐ **HIGH** ☐	**CALLED** ☐
DATE: **TIME:**	**MESSAGE:**
NAME:	
COMPANY:	
PHONE:	
EMAIL:	
IMPORTANCE: LOW ☐ **MEDIUM** ☐ **HIGH** ☐	**CALLED** ☐
DATE: **TIME:**	**MESSAGE:**
NAME:	
COMPANY:	
PHONE:	
EMAIL:	
IMPORTANCE: LOW ☐ **MEDIUM** ☐ **HIGH** ☐	**CALLED** ☐
DATE: **TIME:**	**MESSAGE:**
NAME:	
COMPANY:	
PHONE:	
EMAIL:	
IMPORTANCE: LOW ☐ **MEDIUM** ☐ **HIGH** ☐	**CALLED** ☐

DATE: TIME:	MESSAGE:
NAME:	
COMPANY:	
PHONE:	
EMAIL:	
IMPORTANCE: LOW ☐ MEDIUM ☐ HIGH ☐	CALLED ☐

DATE: TIME:	MESSAGE:
NAME:	
COMPANY:	
PHONE:	
EMAIL:	
IMPORTANCE: LOW ☐ MEDIUM ☐ HIGH ☐	CALLED ☐

DATE: TIME:	MESSAGE:
NAME:	
COMPANY:	
PHONE:	
EMAIL:	
IMPORTANCE: LOW ☐ MEDIUM ☐ HIGH ☐	CALLED ☐

DATE: TIME:	MESSAGE:
NAME:	
COMPANY:	
PHONE:	
EMAIL:	
IMPORTANCE: LOW ☐ MEDIUM ☐ HIGH ☐	CALLED ☐

DATE: TIME:	MESSAGE:
NAME:	
COMPANY:	
PHONE:	
EMAIL:	
IMPORTANCE: LOW ☐ MEDIUM ☐ HIGH ☐	CALLED ☐

DATE: **TIME:**	**MESSAGE:**
NAME:	
COMPANY:	
PHONE:	
EMAIL:	
IMPORTANCE: LOW ☐ **MEDIUM** ☐ **HIGH** ☐	**CALLED** ☐
DATE: **TIME:**	**MESSAGE:**
NAME:	
COMPANY:	
PHONE:	
EMAIL:	
IMPORTANCE: LOW ☐ **MEDIUM** ☐ **HIGH** ☐	**CALLED** ☐
DATE: **TIME:**	**MESSAGE:**
NAME:	
COMPANY:	
PHONE:	
EMAIL:	
IMPORTANCE: LOW ☐ **MEDIUM** ☐ **HIGH** ☐	**CALLED** ☐
DATE: **TIME:**	**MESSAGE:**
NAME:	
COMPANY:	
PHONE:	
EMAIL:	
IMPORTANCE: LOW ☐ **MEDIUM** ☐ **HIGH** ☐	**CALLED** ☐
DATE: **TIME:**	**MESSAGE:**
NAME:	
COMPANY:	
PHONE:	
EMAIL:	
IMPORTANCE: LOW ☐ **MEDIUM** ☐ **HIGH** ☐	**CALLED** ☐

DATE:　　　　**TIME:**	**MESSAGE:**
NAME:	
COMPANY:	
PHONE:	
EMAIL:	
IMPORTANCE: LOW ☐ **MEDIUM** ☐ **HIGH** ☐	**CALLED** ☐
DATE:　　　　**TIME:**	**MESSAGE:**
NAME:	
COMPANY:	
PHONE:	
EMAIL:	
IMPORTANCE: LOW ☐ **MEDIUM** ☐ **HIGH** ☐	**CALLED** ☐
DATE:　　　　**TIME:**	**MESSAGE:**
NAME:	
COMPANY:	
PHONE:	
EMAIL:	
IMPORTANCE: LOW ☐ **MEDIUM** ☐ **HIGH** ☐	**CALLED** ☐
DATE:　　　　**TIME:**	**MESSAGE:**
NAME:	
COMPANY:	
PHONE:	
EMAIL:	
IMPORTANCE: LOW ☐ **MEDIUM** ☐ **HIGH** ☐	**CALLED** ☐
DATE:　　　　**TIME:**	**MESSAGE:**
NAME:	
COMPANY:	
PHONE:	
EMAIL:	
IMPORTANCE: LOW ☐ **MEDIUM** ☐ **HIGH** ☐	**CALLED** ☐

DATE: **TIME:**	**MESSAGE:**
NAME:	
COMPANY:	
PHONE:	
EMAIL:	
IMPORTANCE: LOW ☐ **MEDIUM** ☐ **HIGH** ☐	**CALLED** ☐
DATE: **TIME:**	**MESSAGE:**
NAME:	
COMPANY:	
PHONE:	
EMAIL:	
IMPORTANCE: LOW ☐ **MEDIUM** ☐ **HIGH** ☐	**CALLED** ☐
DATE: **TIME:**	**MESSAGE:**
NAME:	
COMPANY:	
PHONE:	
EMAIL:	
IMPORTANCE: LOW ☐ **MEDIUM** ☐ **HIGH** ☐	**CALLED** ☐
DATE: **TIME:**	**MESSAGE:**
NAME:	
COMPANY:	
PHONE:	
EMAIL:	
IMPORTANCE: LOW ☐ **MEDIUM** ☐ **HIGH** ☐	**CALLED** ☐
DATE: **TIME:**	**MESSAGE:**
NAME:	
COMPANY:	
PHONE:	
EMAIL:	
IMPORTANCE: LOW ☐ **MEDIUM** ☐ **HIGH** ☐	**CALLED** ☐

DATE: TIME:	MESSAGE:
NAME:	
COMPANY:	
PHONE:	
EMAIL:	
IMPORTANCE: LOW ☐ MEDIUM ☐ HIGH ☐	CALLED ☐
DATE: TIME:	MESSAGE:
NAME:	
COMPANY:	
PHONE:	
EMAIL:	
IMPORTANCE: LOW ☐ MEDIUM ☐ HIGH ☐	CALLED ☐
DATE: TIME:	MESSAGE:
NAME:	
COMPANY:	
PHONE:	
EMAIL:	
IMPORTANCE: LOW ☐ MEDIUM ☐ HIGH ☐	CALLED ☐
DATE: TIME:	MESSAGE:
NAME:	
COMPANY:	
PHONE:	
EMAIL:	
IMPORTANCE: LOW ☐ MEDIUM ☐ HIGH ☐	CALLED ☐
DATE: TIME:	MESSAGE:
NAME:	
COMPANY:	
PHONE:	
EMAIL:	
IMPORTANCE: LOW ☐ MEDIUM ☐ HIGH ☐	CALLED ☐

DATE: **TIME:**	**MESSAGE:**
NAME:	
COMPANY:	
PHONE:	
EMAIL:	
IMPORTANCE: LOW ☐ **MEDIUM** ☐ **HIGH** ☐	**CALLED** ☐
DATE: **TIME:**	**MESSAGE:**
NAME:	
COMPANY:	
PHONE:	
EMAIL:	
IMPORTANCE: LOW ☐ **MEDIUM** ☐ **HIGH** ☐	**CALLED** ☐
DATE: **TIME:**	**MESSAGE:**
NAME:	
COMPANY:	
PHONE:	
EMAIL:	
IMPORTANCE: LOW ☐ **MEDIUM** ☐ **HIGH** ☐	**CALLED** ☐
DATE: **TIME:**	**MESSAGE:**
NAME:	
COMPANY:	
PHONE:	
EMAIL:	
IMPORTANCE: LOW ☐ **MEDIUM** ☐ **HIGH** ☐	**CALLED** ☐
DATE: **TIME:**	**MESSAGE:**
NAME:	
COMPANY:	
PHONE:	
EMAIL:	
IMPORTANCE: LOW ☐ **MEDIUM** ☐ **HIGH** ☐	**CALLED** ☐

DATE: **TIME:**	**MESSAGE:**
NAME:	
COMPANY:	
PHONE:	
EMAIL:	
IMPORTANCE: LOW ☐ **MEDIUM** ☐ **HIGH** ☐	**CALLED** ☐
DATE: **TIME:**	**MESSAGE:**
NAME:	
COMPANY:	
PHONE:	
EMAIL:	
IMPORTANCE: LOW ☐ **MEDIUM** ☐ **HIGH** ☐	**CALLED** ☐
DATE: **TIME:**	**MESSAGE:**
NAME:	
COMPANY:	
PHONE:	
EMAIL:	
IMPORTANCE: LOW ☐ **MEDIUM** ☐ **HIGH** ☐	**CALLED** ☐
DATE: **TIME:**	**MESSAGE:**
NAME:	
COMPANY:	
PHONE:	
EMAIL:	
IMPORTANCE: LOW ☐ **MEDIUM** ☐ **HIGH** ☐	**CALLED** ☐
DATE: **TIME:**	**MESSAGE:**
NAME:	
COMPANY:	
PHONE:	
EMAIL:	
IMPORTANCE: LOW ☐ **MEDIUM** ☐ **HIGH** ☐	**CALLED** ☐

DATE: **TIME:**	**MESSAGE:**
NAME:	
COMPANY:	
PHONE:	
EMAIL:	
IMPORTANCE: LOW ☐ **MEDIUM** ☐ **HIGH** ☐	**CALLED** ☐
DATE: **TIME:**	**MESSAGE:**
NAME:	
COMPANY:	
PHONE:	
EMAIL:	
IMPORTANCE: LOW ☐ **MEDIUM** ☐ **HIGH** ☐	**CALLED** ☐
DATE: **TIME:**	**MESSAGE:**
NAME:	
COMPANY:	
PHONE:	
EMAIL:	
IMPORTANCE: LOW ☐ **MEDIUM** ☐ **HIGH** ☐	**CALLED** ☐
DATE: **TIME:**	**MESSAGE:**
NAME:	
COMPANY:	
PHONE:	
EMAIL:	
IMPORTANCE: LOW ☐ **MEDIUM** ☐ **HIGH** ☐	**CALLED** ☐
DATE: **TIME:**	**MESSAGE:**
NAME:	
COMPANY:	
PHONE:	
EMAIL:	
IMPORTANCE: LOW ☐ **MEDIUM** ☐ **HIGH** ☐	**CALLED** ☐

DATE:　　　　　**TIME:**	**MESSAGE:**
NAME:	
COMPANY:	
PHONE:	
EMAIL:	
IMPORTANCE: LOW ☐ **MEDIUM** ☐ **HIGH** ☐	**CALLED** ☐
DATE:　　　　　**TIME:**	**MESSAGE:**
NAME:	
COMPANY:	
PHONE:	
EMAIL:	
IMPORTANCE: LOW ☐ **MEDIUM** ☐ **HIGH** ☐	**CALLED** ☐
DATE:　　　　　**TIME:**	**MESSAGE:**
NAME:	
COMPANY:	
PHONE:	
EMAIL:	
IMPORTANCE: LOW ☐ **MEDIUM** ☐ **HIGH** ☐	**CALLED** ☐
DATE:　　　　　**TIME:**	**MESSAGE:**
NAME:	
COMPANY:	
PHONE:	
EMAIL:	
IMPORTANCE: LOW ☐ **MEDIUM** ☐ **HIGH** ☐	**CALLED** ☐
DATE:　　　　　**TIME:**	**MESSAGE:**
NAME:	
COMPANY:	
PHONE:	
EMAIL:	
IMPORTANCE: LOW ☐ **MEDIUM** ☐ **HIGH** ☐	**CALLED** ☐

DATE:	TIME:	MESSAGE:
NAME:		
COMPANY:		
PHONE:		
EMAIL:		
IMPORTANCE: LOW ▢ MEDIUM ▢ HIGH ▢		CALLED ▢

DATE:	TIME:	MESSAGE:
NAME:		
COMPANY:		
PHONE:		
EMAIL:		
IMPORTANCE: LOW ▢ MEDIUM ▢ HIGH ▢		CALLED ▢

DATE:	TIME:	MESSAGE:
NAME:		
COMPANY:		
PHONE:		
EMAIL:		
IMPORTANCE: LOW ▢ MEDIUM ▢ HIGH ▢		CALLED ▢

DATE:	TIME:	MESSAGE:
NAME:		
COMPANY:		
PHONE:		
EMAIL:		
IMPORTANCE: LOW ▢ MEDIUM ▢ HIGH ▢		CALLED ▢

DATE:	TIME:	MESSAGE:
NAME:		
COMPANY:		
PHONE:		
EMAIL:		
IMPORTANCE: LOW ▢ MEDIUM ▢ HIGH ▢		CALLED ▢

DATE: **TIME:**	**MESSAGE:**
NAME:	
COMPANY:	
PHONE:	
EMAIL:	
IMPORTANCE: LOW ☐ **MEDIUM** ☐ **HIGH** ☐	**CALLED** ☐
DATE: **TIME:**	**MESSAGE:**
NAME:	
COMPANY:	
PHONE:	
EMAIL:	
IMPORTANCE: LOW ☐ **MEDIUM** ☐ **HIGH** ☐	**CALLED** ☐
DATE: **TIME:**	**MESSAGE:**
NAME:	
COMPANY:	
PHONE:	
EMAIL:	
IMPORTANCE: LOW ☐ **MEDIUM** ☐ **HIGH** ☐	**CALLED** ☐
DATE: **TIME:**	**MESSAGE:**
NAME:	
COMPANY:	
PHONE:	
EMAIL:	
IMPORTANCE: LOW ☐ **MEDIUM** ☐ **HIGH** ☐	**CALLED** ☐
DATE: **TIME:**	**MESSAGE:**
NAME:	
COMPANY:	
PHONE:	
EMAIL:	
IMPORTANCE: LOW ☐ **MEDIUM** ☐ **HIGH** ☐	**CALLED** ☐

DATE: **TIME:**	**MESSAGE:**
NAME:	
COMPANY:	
PHONE:	
EMAIL:	
IMPORTANCE: LOW ☐ **MEDIUM** ☐ **HIGH** ☐	**CALLED** ☐
DATE: **TIME:**	**MESSAGE:**
NAME:	
COMPANY:	
PHONE:	
EMAIL:	
IMPORTANCE: LOW ☐ **MEDIUM** ☐ **HIGH** ☐	**CALLED** ☐
DATE: **TIME:**	**MESSAGE:**
NAME:	
COMPANY:	
PHONE:	
EMAIL:	
IMPORTANCE: LOW ☐ **MEDIUM** ☐ **HIGH** ☐	**CALLED** ☐
DATE: **TIME:**	**MESSAGE:**
NAME:	
COMPANY:	
PHONE:	
EMAIL:	
IMPORTANCE: LOW ☐ **MEDIUM** ☐ **HIGH** ☐	**CALLED** ☐
DATE: **TIME:**	**MESSAGE:**
NAME:	
COMPANY:	
PHONE:	
EMAIL:	
IMPORTANCE: LOW ☐ **MEDIUM** ☐ **HIGH** ☐	**CALLED** ☐

DATE: **TIME:**	**MESSAGE:**
NAME:	
COMPANY:	
PHONE:	
EMAIL:	
IMPORTANCE: LOW ▩ **MEDIUM** ▩ **HIGH** ▩	**CALLED** ▩
DATE: **TIME:**	**MESSAGE:**
NAME:	
COMPANY:	
PHONE:	
EMAIL:	
IMPORTANCE: LOW ▩ **MEDIUM** ▩ **HIGH** ▩	**CALLED** ▩
DATE: **TIME:**	**MESSAGE:**
NAME:	
COMPANY:	
PHONE:	
EMAIL:	
IMPORTANCE: LOW ▩ **MEDIUM** ▩ **HIGH** ▩	**CALLED** ▩
DATE: **TIME:**	**MESSAGE:**
NAME:	
COMPANY:	
PHONE:	
EMAIL:	
IMPORTANCE: LOW ▩ **MEDIUM** ▩ **HIGH** ▩	**CALLED** ▩
DATE: **TIME:**	**MESSAGE:**
NAME:	
COMPANY:	
PHONE:	
EMAIL:	
IMPORTANCE: LOW ▩ **MEDIUM** ▩ **HIGH** ▩	**CALLED** ▩

DATE:	TIME:	MESSAGE:
NAME:		
COMPANY:		
PHONE:		
EMAIL:		
IMPORTANCE: LOW ☐ MEDIUM ☐ HIGH ☐		CALLED ☐

DATE:	TIME:	MESSAGE:
NAME:		
COMPANY:		
PHONE:		
EMAIL:		
IMPORTANCE: LOW ☐ MEDIUM ☐ HIGH ☐		CALLED ☐

DATE:	TIME:	MESSAGE:
NAME:		
COMPANY:		
PHONE:		
EMAIL:		
IMPORTANCE: LOW ☐ MEDIUM ☐ HIGH ☐		CALLED ☐

DATE:	TIME:	MESSAGE:
NAME:		
COMPANY:		
PHONE:		
EMAIL:		
IMPORTANCE: LOW ☐ MEDIUM ☐ HIGH ☐		CALLED ☐

DATE:	TIME:	MESSAGE:
NAME:		
COMPANY:		
PHONE:		
EMAIL:		
IMPORTANCE: LOW ☐ MEDIUM ☐ HIGH ☐		CALLED ☐

DATE:　　　　　　　**TIME:**	**MESSAGE:**
NAME:	
COMPANY:	
PHONE:	
EMAIL:	
IMPORTANCE: LOW ☐ **MEDIUM** ☐ **HIGH** ☐	**CALLED** ☐
DATE:　　　　　　　**TIME:**	**MESSAGE:**
NAME:	
COMPANY:	
PHONE:	
EMAIL:	
IMPORTANCE: LOW ☐ **MEDIUM** ☐ **HIGH** ☐	**CALLED** ☐
DATE:　　　　　　　**TIME:**	**MESSAGE:**
NAME:	
COMPANY:	
PHONE:	
EMAIL:	
IMPORTANCE: LOW ☐ **MEDIUM** ☐ **HIGH** ☐	**CALLED** ☐
DATE:　　　　　　　**TIME:**	**MESSAGE:**
NAME:	
COMPANY:	
PHONE:	
EMAIL:	
IMPORTANCE: LOW ☐ **MEDIUM** ☐ **HIGH** ☐	**CALLED** ☐
DATE:　　　　　　　**TIME:**	**MESSAGE:**
NAME:	
COMPANY:	
PHONE:	
EMAIL:	
IMPORTANCE: LOW ☐ **MEDIUM** ☐ **HIGH** ☐	**CALLED** ☐

DATE:	TIME:	MESSAGE:
NAME:		
COMPANY:		
PHONE:		
EMAIL:		
IMPORTANCE: LOW ☐ MEDIUM ☐ HIGH ☐		CALLED ☐

DATE:	TIME:	MESSAGE:
NAME:		
COMPANY:		
PHONE:		
EMAIL:		
IMPORTANCE: LOW ☐ MEDIUM ☐ HIGH ☐		CALLED ☐

DATE:	TIME:	MESSAGE:
NAME:		
COMPANY:		
PHONE:		
EMAIL:		
IMPORTANCE: LOW ☐ MEDIUM ☐ HIGH ☐		CALLED ☐

DATE:	TIME:	MESSAGE:
NAME:		
COMPANY:		
PHONE:		
EMAIL:		
IMPORTANCE: LOW ☐ MEDIUM ☐ HIGH ☐		CALLED ☐

DATE:	TIME:	MESSAGE:
NAME:		
COMPANY:		
PHONE:		
EMAIL:		
IMPORTANCE: LOW ☐ MEDIUM ☐ HIGH ☐		CALLED ☐

DATE: **TIME:**	**MESSAGE:**
NAME:	
COMPANY:	
PHONE:	
EMAIL:	
IMPORTANCE: LOW ☐ **MEDIUM** ☐ **HIGH** ☐	**CALLED** ☐
DATE: **TIME:**	**MESSAGE:**
NAME:	
COMPANY:	
PHONE:	
EMAIL:	
IMPORTANCE: LOW ☐ **MEDIUM** ☐ **HIGH** ☐	**CALLED** ☐
DATE: **TIME:**	**MESSAGE:**
NAME:	
COMPANY:	
PHONE:	
EMAIL:	
IMPORTANCE: LOW ☐ **MEDIUM** ☐ **HIGH** ☐	**CALLED** ☐
DATE: **TIME:**	**MESSAGE:**
NAME:	
COMPANY:	
PHONE:	
EMAIL:	
IMPORTANCE: LOW ☐ **MEDIUM** ☐ **HIGH** ☐	**CALLED** ☐
DATE: **TIME:**	**MESSAGE:**
NAME:	
COMPANY:	
PHONE:	
EMAIL:	
IMPORTANCE: LOW ☐ **MEDIUM** ☐ **HIGH** ☐	**CALLED** ☐

DATE: **TIME:**	**MESSAGE:**
NAME:	
COMPANY:	
PHONE:	
EMAIL:	
IMPORTANCE: LOW ☐ **MEDIUM** ☐ **HIGH** ☐	**CALLED** ☐
DATE: **TIME:**	**MESSAGE:**
NAME:	
COMPANY:	
PHONE:	
EMAIL:	
IMPORTANCE: LOW ☐ **MEDIUM** ☐ **HIGH** ☐	**CALLED** ☐
DATE: **TIME:**	**MESSAGE:**
NAME:	
COMPANY:	
PHONE:	
EMAIL:	
IMPORTANCE: LOW ☐ **MEDIUM** ☐ **HIGH** ☐	**CALLED** ☐
DATE: **TIME:**	**MESSAGE:**
NAME:	
COMPANY:	
PHONE:	
EMAIL:	
IMPORTANCE: LOW ☐ **MEDIUM** ☐ **HIGH** ☐	**CALLED** ☐
DATE: **TIME:**	**MESSAGE:**
NAME:	
COMPANY:	
PHONE:	
EMAIL:	
IMPORTANCE: LOW ☐ **MEDIUM** ☐ **HIGH** ☐	**CALLED** ☐

DATE:　　　　　　**TIME:**	**MESSAGE:**
NAME:	
COMPANY:	
PHONE:	
EMAIL:	
IMPORTANCE: LOW ☐　MEDIUM ☐　HIGH ☐	**CALLED** ☐
DATE:　　　　　　**TIME:**	**MESSAGE:**
NAME:	
COMPANY:	
PHONE:	
EMAIL:	
IMPORTANCE: LOW ☐　MEDIUM ☐　HIGH ☐	**CALLED** ☐
DATE:　　　　　　**TIME:**	**MESSAGE:**
NAME:	
COMPANY:	
PHONE:	
EMAIL:	
IMPORTANCE: LOW ☐　MEDIUM ☐　HIGH ☐	**CALLED** ☐
DATE:　　　　　　**TIME:**	**MESSAGE:**
NAME:	
COMPANY:	
PHONE:	
EMAIL:	
IMPORTANCE: LOW ☐　MEDIUM ☐　HIGH ☐	**CALLED** ☐
DATE:　　　　　　**TIME:**	**MESSAGE:**
NAME:	
COMPANY:	
PHONE:	
EMAIL:	
IMPORTANCE: LOW ☐　MEDIUM ☐　HIGH ☐	**CALLED** ☐

	MESSAGE:
DATE: **TIME:**	
NAME:	
COMPANY:	
PHONE:	
EMAIL:	
IMPORTANCE: LOW ☐ **MEDIUM** ☐ **HIGH** ☐	**CALLED** ☐
DATE: **TIME:**	**MESSAGE:**
NAME:	
COMPANY:	
PHONE:	
EMAIL:	
IMPORTANCE: LOW ☐ **MEDIUM** ☐ **HIGH** ☐	**CALLED** ☐
DATE: **TIME:**	**MESSAGE:**
NAME:	
COMPANY:	
PHONE:	
EMAIL:	
IMPORTANCE: LOW ☐ **MEDIUM** ☐ **HIGH** ☐	**CALLED** ☐
DATE: **TIME:**	**MESSAGE:**
NAME:	
COMPANY:	
PHONE:	
EMAIL:	
IMPORTANCE: LOW ☐ **MEDIUM** ☐ **HIGH** ☐	**CALLED** ☐
DATE: **TIME:**	**MESSAGE:**
NAME:	
COMPANY:	
PHONE:	
EMAIL:	
IMPORTANCE: LOW ☐ **MEDIUM** ☐ **HIGH** ☐	**CALLED** ☐

DATE: **TIME:**	**MESSAGE:**
NAME:	
COMPANY:	
PHONE:	
EMAIL:	
IMPORTANCE: LOW ☐ **MEDIUM** ☐ **HIGH** ☐	**CALLED** ☐
DATE: **TIME:**	**MESSAGE:**
NAME:	
COMPANY:	
PHONE:	
EMAIL:	
IMPORTANCE: LOW ☐ **MEDIUM** ☐ **HIGH** ☐	**CALLED** ☐
DATE: **TIME:**	**MESSAGE:**
NAME:	
COMPANY:	
PHONE:	
EMAIL:	
IMPORTANCE: LOW ☐ **MEDIUM** ☐ **HIGH** ☐	**CALLED** ☐
DATE: **TIME:**	**MESSAGE:**
NAME:	
COMPANY:	
PHONE:	
EMAIL:	
IMPORTANCE: LOW ☐ **MEDIUM** ☐ **HIGH** ☐	**CALLED** ☐
DATE: **TIME:**	**MESSAGE:**
NAME:	
COMPANY:	
PHONE:	
EMAIL:	
IMPORTANCE: LOW ☐ **MEDIUM** ☐ **HIGH** ☐	**CALLED** ☐

DATE: **TIME:**	**MESSAGE:**
NAME:	
COMPANY:	
PHONE:	
EMAIL:	
IMPORTANCE: LOW ☐ MEDIUM ☐ HIGH ☐	**CALLED ☐**
DATE: **TIME:**	**MESSAGE:**
NAME:	
COMPANY:	
PHONE:	
EMAIL:	
IMPORTANCE: LOW ☐ MEDIUM ☐ HIGH ☐	**CALLED ☐**
DATE: **TIME:**	**MESSAGE:**
NAME:	
COMPANY:	
PHONE:	
EMAIL:	
IMPORTANCE: LOW ☐ MEDIUM ☐ HIGH ☐	**CALLED ☐**
DATE: **TIME:**	**MESSAGE:**
NAME:	
COMPANY:	
PHONE:	
EMAIL:	
IMPORTANCE: LOW ☐ MEDIUM ☐ HIGH ☐	**CALLED ☐**
DATE: **TIME:**	**MESSAGE:**
NAME:	
COMPANY:	
PHONE:	
EMAIL:	
IMPORTANCE: LOW ☐ MEDIUM ☐ HIGH ☐	**CALLED ☐**

	MESSAGE:
DATE:　　　　　　**TIME:**	
NAME:	
COMPANY:	
PHONE:	
EMAIL:	
IMPORTANCE: LOW ☐　MEDIUM ☐　HIGH ☐	**CALLED** ☐

	MESSAGE:
DATE:　　　　　　**TIME:**	
NAME:	
COMPANY:	
PHONE:	
EMAIL:	
IMPORTANCE: LOW ☐　MEDIUM ☐　HIGH ☐	**CALLED** ☐

	MESSAGE:
DATE:　　　　　　**TIME:**	
NAME:	
COMPANY:	
PHONE:	
EMAIL:	
IMPORTANCE: LOW ☐　MEDIUM ☐　HIGH ☐	**CALLED** ☐

	MESSAGE:
DATE:　　　　　　**TIME:**	
NAME:	
COMPANY:	
PHONE:	
EMAIL:	
IMPORTANCE: LOW ☐　MEDIUM ☐　HIGH ☐	**CALLED** ☐

	MESSAGE:
DATE:　　　　　　**TIME:**	
NAME:	
COMPANY:	
PHONE:	
EMAIL:	
IMPORTANCE: LOW ☐　MEDIUM ☐　HIGH ☐	**CALLED** ☐

DATE: **TIME:**	**MESSAGE:**
NAME:	
COMPANY:	
PHONE:	
EMAIL:	
IMPORTANCE: LOW ▢ **MEDIUM** ▢ **HIGH** ▢	**CALLED** ▢
DATE: **TIME:**	**MESSAGE:**
NAME:	
COMPANY:	
PHONE:	
EMAIL:	
IMPORTANCE: LOW ▢ **MEDIUM** ▢ **HIGH** ▢	**CALLED** ▢
DATE: **TIME:**	**MESSAGE:**
NAME:	
COMPANY:	
PHONE:	
EMAIL:	
IMPORTANCE: LOW ▢ **MEDIUM** ▢ **HIGH** ▢	**CALLED** ▢
DATE: **TIME:**	**MESSAGE:**
NAME:	
COMPANY:	
PHONE:	
EMAIL:	
IMPORTANCE: LOW ▢ **MEDIUM** ▢ **HIGH** ▢	**CALLED** ▢
DATE: **TIME:**	**MESSAGE:**
NAME:	
COMPANY:	
PHONE:	
EMAIL:	
IMPORTANCE: LOW ▢ **MEDIUM** ▢ **HIGH** ▢	**CALLED** ▢

DATE: **TIME:**	**MESSAGE:**
NAME:	
COMPANY:	
PHONE:	
EMAIL:	
IMPORTANCE: LOW ☐ **MEDIUM** ☐ **HIGH** ☐	**CALLED** ☐
DATE: **TIME:**	**MESSAGE:**
NAME:	
COMPANY:	
PHONE:	
EMAIL:	
IMPORTANCE: LOW ☐ **MEDIUM** ☐ **HIGH** ☐	**CALLED** ☐
DATE: **TIME:**	**MESSAGE:**
NAME:	
COMPANY:	
PHONE:	
EMAIL:	
IMPORTANCE: LOW ☐ **MEDIUM** ☐ **HIGH** ☐	**CALLED** ☐
DATE: **TIME:**	**MESSAGE:**
NAME:	
COMPANY:	
PHONE:	
EMAIL:	
IMPORTANCE: LOW ☐ **MEDIUM** ☐ **HIGH** ☐	**CALLED** ☐
DATE: **TIME:**	**MESSAGE:**
NAME:	
COMPANY:	
PHONE:	
EMAIL:	
IMPORTANCE: LOW ☐ **MEDIUM** ☐ **HIGH** ☐	**CALLED** ☐

DATE: TIME:	MESSAGE:
NAME:	
COMPANY:	
PHONE:	
EMAIL:	
IMPORTANCE: LOW ☐ MEDIUM ☐ HIGH ☐	CALLED ☐
DATE: TIME:	MESSAGE:
NAME:	
COMPANY:	
PHONE:	
EMAIL:	
IMPORTANCE: LOW ☐ MEDIUM ☐ HIGH ☐	CALLED ☐
DATE: TIME:	MESSAGE:
NAME:	
COMPANY:	
PHONE:	
EMAIL:	
IMPORTANCE: LOW ☐ MEDIUM ☐ HIGH ☐	CALLED ☐
DATE: TIME:	MESSAGE:
NAME:	
COMPANY:	
PHONE:	
EMAIL:	
IMPORTANCE: LOW ☐ MEDIUM ☐ HIGH ☐	CALLED ☐
DATE: TIME:	MESSAGE:
NAME:	
COMPANY:	
PHONE:	
EMAIL:	
IMPORTANCE: LOW ☐ MEDIUM ☐ HIGH ☐	CALLED ☐

	MESSAGE:
DATE: TIME:	
NAME:	
COMPANY:	
PHONE:	
EMAIL:	
IMPORTANCE: LOW ☐ MEDIUM ☐ HIGH ☐	CALLED ☐
DATE: TIME:	MESSAGE:
NAME:	
COMPANY:	
PHONE:	
EMAIL:	
IMPORTANCE: LOW ☐ MEDIUM ☐ HIGH ☐	CALLED ☐
DATE: TIME:	MESSAGE:
NAME:	
COMPANY:	
PHONE:	
EMAIL:	
IMPORTANCE: LOW ☐ MEDIUM ☐ HIGH ☐	CALLED ☐
DATE: TIME:	MESSAGE:
NAME:	
COMPANY:	
PHONE:	
EMAIL:	
IMPORTANCE: LOW ☐ MEDIUM ☐ HIGH ☐	CALLED ☐
DATE: TIME:	MESSAGE:
NAME:	
COMPANY:	
PHONE:	
EMAIL:	
IMPORTANCE: LOW ☐ MEDIUM ☐ HIGH ☐	CALLED ☐

DATE: **TIME:**	**MESSAGE:**
NAME:	
COMPANY:	
PHONE:	
EMAIL:	
IMPORTANCE: LOW ☐ **MEDIUM** ☐ **HIGH** ☐	**CALLED** ☐
DATE: **TIME:**	**MESSAGE:**
NAME:	
COMPANY:	
PHONE:	
EMAIL:	
IMPORTANCE: LOW ☐ **MEDIUM** ☐ **HIGH** ☐	**CALLED** ☐
DATE: **TIME:**	**MESSAGE:**
NAME:	
COMPANY:	
PHONE:	
EMAIL:	
IMPORTANCE: LOW ☐ **MEDIUM** ☐ **HIGH** ☐	**CALLED** ☐
DATE: **TIME:**	**MESSAGE:**
NAME:	
COMPANY:	
PHONE:	
EMAIL:	
IMPORTANCE: LOW ☐ **MEDIUM** ☐ **HIGH** ☐	**CALLED** ☐
DATE: **TIME:**	**MESSAGE:**
NAME:	
COMPANY:	
PHONE:	
EMAIL:	
IMPORTANCE: LOW ☐ **MEDIUM** ☐ **HIGH** ☐	**CALLED** ☐

DATE: **TIME:**	**MESSAGE:**
NAME:	
COMPANY:	
PHONE:	
EMAIL:	
IMPORTANCE: LOW ☐ **MEDIUM** ☐ **HIGH** ☐	**CALLED** ☐
DATE: **TIME:**	**MESSAGE:**
NAME:	
COMPANY:	
PHONE:	
EMAIL:	
IMPORTANCE: LOW ☐ **MEDIUM** ☐ **HIGH** ☐	**CALLED** ☐
DATE: **TIME:**	**MESSAGE:**
NAME:	
COMPANY:	
PHONE:	
EMAIL:	
IMPORTANCE: LOW ☐ **MEDIUM** ☐ **HIGH** ☐	**CALLED** ☐
DATE: **TIME:**	**MESSAGE:**
NAME:	
COMPANY:	
PHONE:	
EMAIL:	
IMPORTANCE: LOW ☐ **MEDIUM** ☐ **HIGH** ☐	**CALLED** ☐
DATE: **TIME:**	**MESSAGE:**
NAME:	
COMPANY:	
PHONE:	
EMAIL:	
IMPORTANCE: LOW ☐ **MEDIUM** ☐ **HIGH** ☐	**CALLED** ☐

DATE: **TIME:**	**MESSAGE:**
NAME:	
COMPANY:	
PHONE:	
EMAIL:	
IMPORTANCE: LOW ☐ MEDIUM ☐ HIGH ☐	**CALLED** ☐
DATE: **TIME:**	**MESSAGE:**
NAME:	
COMPANY:	
PHONE:	
EMAIL:	
IMPORTANCE: LOW ☐ MEDIUM ☐ HIGH ☐	**CALLED** ☐
DATE: **TIME:**	**MESSAGE:**
NAME:	
COMPANY:	
PHONE:	
EMAIL:	
IMPORTANCE: LOW ☐ MEDIUM ☐ HIGH ☐	**CALLED** ☐
DATE: **TIME:**	**MESSAGE:**
NAME:	
COMPANY:	
PHONE:	
EMAIL:	
IMPORTANCE: LOW ☐ MEDIUM ☐ HIGH ☐	**CALLED** ☐
DATE: **TIME:**	**MESSAGE:**
NAME:	
COMPANY:	
PHONE:	
EMAIL:	
IMPORTANCE: LOW ☐ MEDIUM ☐ HIGH ☐	**CALLED** ☐

DATE: **TIME:**	**MESSAGE:**
NAME:	
COMPANY:	
PHONE:	
EMAIL:	
IMPORTANCE: LOW ☐ **MEDIUM** ☐ **HIGH** ☐	**CALLED** ☐
DATE: **TIME:**	**MESSAGE:**
NAME:	
COMPANY:	
PHONE:	
EMAIL:	
IMPORTANCE: LOW ☐ **MEDIUM** ☐ **HIGH** ☐	**CALLED** ☐
DATE: **TIME:**	**MESSAGE:**
NAME:	
COMPANY:	
PHONE:	
EMAIL:	
IMPORTANCE: LOW ☐ **MEDIUM** ☐ **HIGH** ☐	**CALLED** ☐
DATE: **TIME:**	**MESSAGE:**
NAME:	
COMPANY:	
PHONE:	
EMAIL:	
IMPORTANCE: LOW ☐ **MEDIUM** ☐ **HIGH** ☐	**CALLED** ☐
DATE: **TIME:**	**MESSAGE:**
NAME:	
COMPANY:	
PHONE:	
EMAIL:	
IMPORTANCE: LOW ☐ **MEDIUM** ☐ **HIGH** ☐	**CALLED** ☐

DATE: **TIME:**	**MESSAGE:**
NAME:	
COMPANY:	
PHONE:	
EMAIL:	
IMPORTANCE: LOW ▢ **MEDIUM** ▢ **HIGH** ▢	**CALLED** ▢
DATE: **TIME:**	**MESSAGE:**
NAME:	
COMPANY:	
PHONE:	
EMAIL:	
IMPORTANCE: LOW ▢ **MEDIUM** ▢ **HIGH** ▢	**CALLED** ▢
DATE: **TIME:**	**MESSAGE:**
NAME:	
COMPANY:	
PHONE:	
EMAIL:	
IMPORTANCE: LOW ▢ **MEDIUM** ▢ **HIGH** ▢	**CALLED** ▢
DATE: **TIME:**	**MESSAGE:**
NAME:	
COMPANY:	
PHONE:	
EMAIL:	
IMPORTANCE: LOW ▢ **MEDIUM** ▢ **HIGH** ▢	**CALLED** ▢
DATE: **TIME:**	**MESSAGE:**
NAME:	
COMPANY:	
PHONE:	
EMAIL:	
IMPORTANCE: LOW ▢ **MEDIUM** ▢ **HIGH** ▢	**CALLED** ▢

DATE:	TIME:	MESSAGE:
NAME:		
COMPANY:		
PHONE:		
EMAIL:		
IMPORTANCE: LOW ☐ MEDIUM ☐ HIGH ☐		**CALLED ☐**

DATE:	TIME:	MESSAGE:
NAME:		
COMPANY:		
PHONE:		
EMAIL:		
IMPORTANCE: LOW ☐ MEDIUM ☐ HIGH ☐		**CALLED ☐**

DATE:	TIME:	MESSAGE:
NAME:		
COMPANY:		
PHONE:		
EMAIL:		
IMPORTANCE: LOW ☐ MEDIUM ☐ HIGH ☐		**CALLED ☐**

DATE:	TIME:	MESSAGE:
NAME:		
COMPANY:		
PHONE:		
EMAIL:		
IMPORTANCE: LOW ☐ MEDIUM ☐ HIGH ☐		**CALLED ☐**

DATE:	TIME:	MESSAGE:
NAME:		
COMPANY:		
PHONE:		
EMAIL:		
IMPORTANCE: LOW ☐ MEDIUM ☐ HIGH ☐		**CALLED ☐**

DATE: TIME:	MESSAGE:
NAME:	
COMPANY:	
PHONE:	
EMAIL:	
IMPORTANCE: LOW ☐ MEDIUM ☐ HIGH ☐	CALLED ☐
DATE: TIME:	MESSAGE:
NAME:	
COMPANY:	
PHONE:	
EMAIL:	
IMPORTANCE: LOW ☐ MEDIUM ☐ HIGH ☐	CALLED ☐
DATE: TIME:	MESSAGE:
NAME:	
COMPANY:	
PHONE:	
EMAIL:	
IMPORTANCE: LOW ☐ MEDIUM ☐ HIGH ☐	CALLED ☐
DATE: TIME:	MESSAGE:
NAME:	
COMPANY:	
PHONE:	
EMAIL:	
IMPORTANCE: LOW ☐ MEDIUM ☐ HIGH ☐	CALLED ☐
DATE: TIME:	MESSAGE:
NAME:	
COMPANY:	
PHONE:	
EMAIL:	
IMPORTANCE: LOW ☐ MEDIUM ☐ HIGH ☐	CALLED ☐

DATE: **TIME:**	**MESSAGE:**
NAME:	
COMPANY:	
PHONE:	
EMAIL:	
IMPORTANCE: LOW ☐ **MEDIUM** ☐ **HIGH** ☐	**CALLED** ☐
DATE: **TIME:**	**MESSAGE:**
NAME:	
COMPANY:	
PHONE:	
EMAIL:	
IMPORTANCE: LOW ☐ **MEDIUM** ☐ **HIGH** ☐	**CALLED** ☐
DATE: **TIME:**	**MESSAGE:**
NAME:	
COMPANY:	
PHONE:	
EMAIL:	
IMPORTANCE: LOW ☐ **MEDIUM** ☐ **HIGH** ☐	**CALLED** ☐
DATE: **TIME:**	**MESSAGE:**
NAME:	
COMPANY:	
PHONE:	
EMAIL:	
IMPORTANCE: LOW ☐ **MEDIUM** ☐ **HIGH** ☐	**CALLED** ☐
DATE: **TIME:**	**MESSAGE:**
NAME:	
COMPANY:	
PHONE:	
EMAIL:	
IMPORTANCE: LOW ☐ **MEDIUM** ☐ **HIGH** ☐	**CALLED** ☐

DATE: **TIME:**	**MESSAGE:**
NAME:	
COMPANY:	
PHONE:	
EMAIL:	
IMPORTANCE: LOW ☐ **MEDIUM** ☐ **HIGH** ☐	**CALLED** ☐
DATE: **TIME:**	**MESSAGE:**
NAME:	
COMPANY:	
PHONE:	
EMAIL:	
IMPORTANCE: LOW ☐ **MEDIUM** ☐ **HIGH** ☐	**CALLED** ☐
DATE: **TIME:**	**MESSAGE:**
NAME:	
COMPANY:	
PHONE:	
EMAIL:	
IMPORTANCE: LOW ☐ **MEDIUM** ☐ **HIGH** ☐	**CALLED** ☐
DATE: **TIME:**	**MESSAGE:**
NAME:	
COMPANY:	
PHONE:	
EMAIL:	
IMPORTANCE: LOW ☐ **MEDIUM** ☐ **HIGH** ☐	**CALLED** ☐
DATE: **TIME:**	**MESSAGE:**
NAME:	
COMPANY:	
PHONE:	
EMAIL:	
IMPORTANCE: LOW ☐ **MEDIUM** ☐ **HIGH** ☐	**CALLED** ☐

DATE: **TIME:**	**MESSAGE:**
NAME:	
COMPANY:	
PHONE:	
EMAIL:	
IMPORTANCE: LOW ☐ **MEDIUM** ☐ **HIGH** ☐	**CALLED** ☐
DATE: **TIME:**	**MESSAGE:**
NAME:	
COMPANY:	
PHONE:	
EMAIL:	
IMPORTANCE: LOW ☐ **MEDIUM** ☐ **HIGH** ☐	**CALLED** ☐
DATE: **TIME:**	**MESSAGE:**
NAME:	
COMPANY:	
PHONE:	
EMAIL:	
IMPORTANCE: LOW ☐ **MEDIUM** ☐ **HIGH** ☐	**CALLED** ☐
DATE: **TIME:**	**MESSAGE:**
NAME:	
COMPANY:	
PHONE:	
EMAIL:	
IMPORTANCE: LOW ☐ **MEDIUM** ☐ **HIGH** ☐	**CALLED** ☐
DATE: **TIME:**	**MESSAGE:**
NAME:	
COMPANY:	
PHONE:	
EMAIL:	
IMPORTANCE: LOW ☐ **MEDIUM** ☐ **HIGH** ☐	**CALLED** ☐

DATE:	TIME:	MESSAGE:
NAME:		
COMPANY:		
PHONE:		
EMAIL:		
IMPORTANCE: LOW ☐ MEDIUM ☐ HIGH ☐		CALLED ☐

DATE:	TIME:	MESSAGE:
NAME:		
COMPANY:		
PHONE:		
EMAIL:		
IMPORTANCE: LOW ☐ MEDIUM ☐ HIGH ☐		CALLED ☐

DATE:	TIME:	MESSAGE:
NAME:		
COMPANY:		
PHONE:		
EMAIL:		
IMPORTANCE: LOW ☐ MEDIUM ☐ HIGH ☐		CALLED ☐

DATE:	TIME:	MESSAGE:
NAME:		
COMPANY:		
PHONE:		
EMAIL:		
IMPORTANCE: LOW ☐ MEDIUM ☐ HIGH ☐		CALLED ☐

DATE:	TIME:	MESSAGE:
NAME:		
COMPANY:		
PHONE:		
EMAIL:		
IMPORTANCE: LOW ☐ MEDIUM ☐ HIGH ☐		CALLED ☐

	MESSAGE:
DATE: TIME:	
NAME:	
COMPANY:	
PHONE:	
EMAIL:	
IMPORTANCE: LOW ☐ MEDIUM ☐ HIGH ☐	CALLED ☐
DATE: TIME:	MESSAGE:
NAME:	
COMPANY:	
PHONE:	
EMAIL:	
IMPORTANCE: LOW ☐ MEDIUM ☐ HIGH ☐	CALLED ☐
DATE: TIME:	MESSAGE:
NAME:	
COMPANY:	
PHONE:	
EMAIL:	
IMPORTANCE: LOW ☐ MEDIUM ☐ HIGH ☐	CALLED ☐
DATE: TIME:	MESSAGE:
NAME:	
COMPANY:	
PHONE:	
EMAIL:	
IMPORTANCE: LOW ☐ MEDIUM ☐ HIGH ☐	CALLED ☐
DATE: TIME:	MESSAGE:
NAME:	
COMPANY:	
PHONE:	
EMAIL:	
IMPORTANCE: LOW ☐ MEDIUM ☐ HIGH ☐	CALLED ☐

DATE: TIME:	MESSAGE:
NAME:	
COMPANY:	
PHONE:	
EMAIL:	
IMPORTANCE: LOW ☐ MEDIUM ☐ HIGH ☐	CALLED ☐
DATE: TIME:	MESSAGE:
NAME:	
COMPANY:	
PHONE:	
EMAIL:	
IMPORTANCE: LOW ☐ MEDIUM ☐ HIGH ☐	CALLED ☐
DATE: TIME:	MESSAGE:
NAME:	
COMPANY:	
PHONE:	
EMAIL:	
IMPORTANCE: LOW ☐ MEDIUM ☐ HIGH ☐	CALLED ☐
DATE: TIME:	MESSAGE:
NAME:	
COMPANY:	
PHONE:	
EMAIL:	
IMPORTANCE: LOW ☐ MEDIUM ☐ HIGH ☐	CALLED ☐
DATE: TIME:	MESSAGE:
NAME:	
COMPANY:	
PHONE:	
EMAIL:	
IMPORTANCE: LOW ☐ MEDIUM ☐ HIGH ☐	CALLED ☐

DATE:	TIME:	MESSAGE:
NAME:		
COMPANY:		
PHONE:		
EMAIL:		
IMPORTANCE: LOW ▢ MEDIUM ▢ HIGH ▢		CALLED ▢

DATE:	TIME:	MESSAGE:
NAME:		
COMPANY:		
PHONE:		
EMAIL:		
IMPORTANCE: LOW ▢ MEDIUM ▢ HIGH ▢		CALLED ▢

DATE:	TIME:	MESSAGE:
NAME:		
COMPANY:		
PHONE:		
EMAIL:		
IMPORTANCE: LOW ▢ MEDIUM ▢ HIGH ▢		CALLED ▢

DATE:	TIME:	MESSAGE:
NAME:		
COMPANY:		
PHONE:		
EMAIL:		
IMPORTANCE: LOW ▢ MEDIUM ▢ HIGH ▢		CALLED ▢

DATE:	TIME:	MESSAGE:
NAME:		
COMPANY:		
PHONE:		
EMAIL:		
IMPORTANCE: LOW ▢ MEDIUM ▢ HIGH ▢		CALLED ▢

DATE: **TIME:**	**MESSAGE:**
NAME:	
COMPANY:	
PHONE:	
EMAIL:	
IMPORTANCE: LOW ☐ **MEDIUM** ☐ **HIGH** ☐	**CALLED** ☐
DATE: **TIME:**	**MESSAGE:**
NAME:	
COMPANY:	
PHONE:	
EMAIL:	
IMPORTANCE: LOW ☐ **MEDIUM** ☐ **HIGH** ☐	**CALLED** ☐
DATE: **TIME:**	**MESSAGE:**
NAME:	
COMPANY:	
PHONE:	
EMAIL:	
IMPORTANCE: LOW ☐ **MEDIUM** ☐ **HIGH** ☐	**CALLED** ☐
DATE: **TIME:**	**MESSAGE:**
NAME:	
COMPANY:	
PHONE:	
EMAIL:	
IMPORTANCE: LOW ☐ **MEDIUM** ☐ **HIGH** ☐	**CALLED** ☐
DATE: **TIME:**	**MESSAGE:**
NAME:	
COMPANY:	
PHONE:	
EMAIL:	
IMPORTANCE: LOW ☐ **MEDIUM** ☐ **HIGH** ☐	**CALLED** ☐

DATE: **TIME:**	**MESSAGE:**
NAME:	
COMPANY:	
PHONE:	
EMAIL:	
IMPORTANCE: LOW ☐ **MEDIUM** ☐ **HIGH** ☐	**CALLED** ☐
DATE: **TIME:**	**MESSAGE:**
NAME:	
COMPANY:	
PHONE:	
EMAIL:	
IMPORTANCE: LOW ☐ **MEDIUM** ☐ **HIGH** ☐	**CALLED** ☐
DATE: **TIME:**	**MESSAGE:**
NAME:	
COMPANY:	
PHONE:	
EMAIL:	
IMPORTANCE: LOW ☐ **MEDIUM** ☐ **HIGH** ☐	**CALLED** ☐
DATE: **TIME:**	**MESSAGE:**
NAME:	
COMPANY:	
PHONE:	
EMAIL:	
IMPORTANCE: LOW ☐ **MEDIUM** ☐ **HIGH** ☐	**CALLED** ☐
DATE: **TIME:**	**MESSAGE:**
NAME:	
COMPANY:	
PHONE:	
EMAIL:	
IMPORTANCE: LOW ☐ **MEDIUM** ☐ **HIGH** ☐	**CALLED** ☐

DATE: **TIME:**	**MESSAGE:**
NAME:	
COMPANY:	
PHONE:	
EMAIL:	
IMPORTANCE: LOW ☐ **MEDIUM** ☐ **HIGH** ☐	**CALLED** ☐
DATE: **TIME:**	**MESSAGE:**
NAME:	
COMPANY:	
PHONE:	
EMAIL:	
IMPORTANCE: LOW ☐ **MEDIUM** ☐ **HIGH** ☐	**CALLED** ☐
DATE: **TIME:**	**MESSAGE:**
NAME:	
COMPANY:	
PHONE:	
EMAIL:	
IMPORTANCE: LOW ☐ **MEDIUM** ☐ **HIGH** ☐	**CALLED** ☐
DATE: **TIME:**	**MESSAGE:**
NAME:	
COMPANY:	
PHONE:	
EMAIL:	
IMPORTANCE: LOW ☐ **MEDIUM** ☐ **HIGH** ☐	**CALLED** ☐
DATE: **TIME:**	**MESSAGE:**
NAME:	
COMPANY:	
PHONE:	
EMAIL:	
IMPORTANCE: LOW ☐ **MEDIUM** ☐ **HIGH** ☐	**CALLED** ☐

DATE: **TIME:**	**MESSAGE:**
NAME:	
COMPANY:	
PHONE:	
EMAIL:	
IMPORTANCE: LOW ▢ **MEDIUM** ▢ **HIGH** ▢	**CALLED** ▢
DATE: **TIME:**	**MESSAGE:**
NAME:	
COMPANY:	
PHONE:	
EMAIL:	
IMPORTANCE: LOW ▢ **MEDIUM** ▢ **HIGH** ▢	**CALLED** ▢
DATE: **TIME:**	**MESSAGE:**
NAME:	
COMPANY:	
PHONE:	
EMAIL:	
IMPORTANCE: LOW ▢ **MEDIUM** ▢ **HIGH** ▢	**CALLED** ▢
DATE: **TIME:**	**MESSAGE:**
NAME:	
COMPANY:	
PHONE:	
EMAIL:	
IMPORTANCE: LOW ▢ **MEDIUM** ▢ **HIGH** ▢	**CALLED** ▢
DATE: **TIME:**	**MESSAGE:**
NAME:	
COMPANY:	
PHONE:	
EMAIL:	
IMPORTANCE: LOW ▢ **MEDIUM** ▢ **HIGH** ▢	**CALLED** ▢

DATE:　　　　　**TIME:**	**MESSAGE:**
NAME:	
COMPANY:	
PHONE:	
EMAIL:	
IMPORTANCE: LOW ☐ **MEDIUM** ☐ **HIGH** ☐	**CALLED** ☐
DATE:　　　　　**TIME:**	**MESSAGE:**
NAME:	
COMPANY:	
PHONE:	
EMAIL:	
IMPORTANCE: LOW ☐ **MEDIUM** ☐ **HIGH** ☐	**CALLED** ☐
DATE:　　　　　**TIME:**	**MESSAGE:**
NAME:	
COMPANY:	
PHONE:	
EMAIL:	
IMPORTANCE: LOW ☐ **MEDIUM** ☐ **HIGH** ☐	**CALLED** ☐
DATE:　　　　　**TIME:**	**MESSAGE:**
NAME:	
COMPANY:	
PHONE:	
EMAIL:	
IMPORTANCE: LOW ☐ **MEDIUM** ☐ **HIGH** ☐	**CALLED** ☐
DATE:　　　　　**TIME:**	**MESSAGE:**
NAME:	
COMPANY:	
PHONE:	
EMAIL:	
IMPORTANCE: LOW ☐ **MEDIUM** ☐ **HIGH** ☐	**CALLED** ☐

DATE:	TIME:	MESSAGE:
NAME:		
COMPANY:		
PHONE:		
EMAIL:		
IMPORTANCE: LOW ☐ **MEDIUM** ☐ **HIGH** ☐		**CALLED** ☐
DATE:	**TIME:**	**MESSAGE:**
NAME:		
COMPANY:		
PHONE:		
EMAIL:		
IMPORTANCE: LOW ☐ **MEDIUM** ☐ **HIGH** ☐		**CALLED** ☐
DATE:	**TIME:**	**MESSAGE:**
NAME:		
COMPANY:		
PHONE:		
EMAIL:		
IMPORTANCE: LOW ☐ **MEDIUM** ☐ **HIGH** ☐		**CALLED** ☐
DATE:	**TIME:**	**MESSAGE:**
NAME:		
COMPANY:		
PHONE:		
EMAIL:		
IMPORTANCE: LOW ☐ **MEDIUM** ☐ **HIGH** ☐		**CALLED** ☐
DATE:	**TIME:**	**MESSAGE:**
NAME:		
COMPANY:		
PHONE:		
EMAIL:		
IMPORTANCE: LOW ☐ **MEDIUM** ☐ **HIGH** ☐		**CALLED** ☐

DATE:	TIME:	MESSAGE:
NAME:		
COMPANY:		
PHONE:		
EMAIL:		
IMPORTANCE: LOW ☐ MEDIUM ☐ HIGH ☐		CALLED ☐

DATE:	TIME:	MESSAGE:
NAME:		
COMPANY:		
PHONE:		
EMAIL:		
IMPORTANCE: LOW ☐ MEDIUM ☐ HIGH ☐		CALLED ☐

DATE:	TIME:	MESSAGE:
NAME:		
COMPANY:		
PHONE:		
EMAIL:		
IMPORTANCE: LOW ☐ MEDIUM ☐ HIGH ☐		CALLED ☐

DATE:	TIME:	MESSAGE:
NAME:		
COMPANY:		
PHONE:		
EMAIL:		
IMPORTANCE: LOW ☐ MEDIUM ☐ HIGH ☐		CALLED ☐

DATE:	TIME:	MESSAGE:
NAME:		
COMPANY:		
PHONE:		
EMAIL:		
IMPORTANCE: LOW ☐ MEDIUM ☐ HIGH ☐		CALLED ☐

DATE:	TIME:	MESSAGE:
NAME:		
COMPANY:		
PHONE:		
EMAIL:		
IMPORTANCE: LOW ☐ **MEDIUM** ☐ **HIGH** ☐		**CALLED** ☐

DATE:	TIME:	MESSAGE:
NAME:		
COMPANY:		
PHONE:		
EMAIL:		
IMPORTANCE: LOW ☐ **MEDIUM** ☐ **HIGH** ☐		**CALLED** ☐

DATE:	TIME:	MESSAGE:
NAME:		
COMPANY:		
PHONE:		
EMAIL:		
IMPORTANCE: LOW ☐ **MEDIUM** ☐ **HIGH** ☐		**CALLED** ☐

DATE:	TIME:	MESSAGE:
NAME:		
COMPANY:		
PHONE:		
EMAIL:		
IMPORTANCE: LOW ☐ **MEDIUM** ☐ **HIGH** ☐		**CALLED** ☐

DATE:	TIME:	MESSAGE:
NAME:		
COMPANY:		
PHONE:		
EMAIL:		
IMPORTANCE: LOW ☐ **MEDIUM** ☐ **HIGH** ☐		**CALLED** ☐

DATE:　　　　　**TIME:**	**MESSAGE:**
NAME:	
COMPANY:	
PHONE:	
EMAIL:	
IMPORTANCE: LOW ☐　MEDIUM ☐　HIGH ☐	**CALLED** ☐
DATE:　　　　　**TIME:**	**MESSAGE:**
NAME:	
COMPANY:	
PHONE:	
EMAIL:	
IMPORTANCE: LOW ☐　MEDIUM ☐　HIGH ☐	**CALLED** ☐
DATE:　　　　　**TIME:**	**MESSAGE:**
NAME:	
COMPANY:	
PHONE:	
EMAIL:	
IMPORTANCE: LOW ☐　MEDIUM ☐　HIGH ☐	**CALLED** ☐
DATE:　　　　　**TIME:**	**MESSAGE:**
NAME:	
COMPANY:	
PHONE:	
EMAIL:	
IMPORTANCE: LOW ☐　MEDIUM ☐　HIGH ☐	**CALLED** ☐
DATE:　　　　　**TIME:**	**MESSAGE:**
NAME:	
COMPANY:	
PHONE:	
EMAIL:	
IMPORTANCE: LOW ☐　MEDIUM ☐　HIGH ☐	**CALLED** ☐

DATE: **TIME:**	**MESSAGE:**
NAME:	
COMPANY:	
PHONE:	
EMAIL:	
IMPORTANCE: LOW ☐ **MEDIUM** ☐ **HIGH** ☐	**CALLED** ☐
DATE: **TIME:**	**MESSAGE:**
NAME:	
COMPANY:	
PHONE:	
EMAIL:	
IMPORTANCE: LOW ☐ **MEDIUM** ☐ **HIGH** ☐	**CALLED** ☐
DATE: **TIME:**	**MESSAGE:**
NAME:	
COMPANY:	
PHONE:	
EMAIL:	
IMPORTANCE: LOW ☐ **MEDIUM** ☐ **HIGH** ☐	**CALLED** ☐
DATE: **TIME:**	**MESSAGE:**
NAME:	
COMPANY:	
PHONE:	
EMAIL:	
IMPORTANCE: LOW ☐ **MEDIUM** ☐ **HIGH** ☐	**CALLED** ☐
DATE: **TIME:**	**MESSAGE:**
NAME:	
COMPANY:	
PHONE:	
EMAIL:	
IMPORTANCE: LOW ☐ **MEDIUM** ☐ **HIGH** ☐	**CALLED** ☐

DATE: TIME:	MESSAGE:
NAME:	
COMPANY:	
PHONE:	
EMAIL:	
IMPORTANCE: LOW ▢ MEDIUM ▢ HIGH ▢	CALLED ▢
DATE: TIME:	MESSAGE:
NAME:	
COMPANY:	
PHONE:	
EMAIL:	
IMPORTANCE: LOW ▢ MEDIUM ▢ HIGH ▢	CALLED ▢
DATE: TIME:	MESSAGE:
NAME:	
COMPANY:	
PHONE:	
EMAIL:	
IMPORTANCE: LOW ▢ MEDIUM ▢ HIGH ▢	CALLED ▢
DATE: TIME:	MESSAGE:
NAME:	
COMPANY:	
PHONE:	
EMAIL:	
IMPORTANCE: LOW ▢ MEDIUM ▢ HIGH ▢	CALLED ▢
DATE: TIME:	MESSAGE:
NAME:	
COMPANY:	
PHONE:	
EMAIL:	
IMPORTANCE: LOW ▢ MEDIUM ▢ HIGH ▢	CALLED ▢

DATE: TIME:	MESSAGE:
NAME:	
COMPANY:	
PHONE:	
EMAIL:	
IMPORTANCE: LOW ☐ MEDIUM ☐ HIGH ☐	CALLED ☐

DATE: TIME:	MESSAGE:
NAME:	
COMPANY:	
PHONE:	
EMAIL:	
IMPORTANCE: LOW ☐ MEDIUM ☐ HIGH ☐	CALLED ☐

DATE: TIME:	MESSAGE:
NAME:	
COMPANY:	
PHONE:	
EMAIL:	
IMPORTANCE: LOW ☐ MEDIUM ☐ HIGH ☐	CALLED ☐

DATE: TIME:	MESSAGE:
NAME:	
COMPANY:	
PHONE:	
EMAIL:	
IMPORTANCE: LOW ☐ MEDIUM ☐ HIGH ☐	CALLED ☐

DATE: TIME:	MESSAGE:
NAME:	
COMPANY:	
PHONE:	
EMAIL:	
IMPORTANCE: LOW ☐ MEDIUM ☐ HIGH ☐	CALLED ☐

	MESSAGE:
DATE: **TIME:**	
NAME:	
COMPANY:	
PHONE:	
EMAIL:	
IMPORTANCE: LOW ☐ **MEDIUM** ☐ **HIGH** ☐	**CALLED** ☐

	MESSAGE:
DATE: **TIME:**	
NAME:	
COMPANY:	
PHONE:	
EMAIL:	
IMPORTANCE: LOW ☐ **MEDIUM** ☐ **HIGH** ☐	**CALLED** ☐

	MESSAGE:
DATE: **TIME:**	
NAME:	
COMPANY:	
PHONE:	
EMAIL:	
IMPORTANCE: LOW ☐ **MEDIUM** ☐ **HIGH** ☐	**CALLED** ☐

	MESSAGE:
DATE: **TIME:**	
NAME:	
COMPANY:	
PHONE:	
EMAIL:	
IMPORTANCE: LOW ☐ **MEDIUM** ☐ **HIGH** ☐	**CALLED** ☐

	MESSAGE:
DATE: **TIME:**	
NAME:	
COMPANY:	
PHONE:	
EMAIL:	
IMPORTANCE: LOW ☐ **MEDIUM** ☐ **HIGH** ☐	**CALLED** ☐

DATE:	TIME:	MESSAGE:
NAME:		
COMPANY:		
PHONE:		
EMAIL:		
IMPORTANCE: LOW ☐ MEDIUM ☐ HIGH ☐		CALLED ☐

DATE:	TIME:	MESSAGE:
NAME:		
COMPANY:		
PHONE:		
EMAIL:		
IMPORTANCE: LOW ☐ MEDIUM ☐ HIGH ☐		CALLED ☐

DATE:	TIME:	MESSAGE:
NAME:		
COMPANY:		
PHONE:		
EMAIL:		
IMPORTANCE: LOW ☐ MEDIUM ☐ HIGH ☐		CALLED ☐

DATE:	TIME:	MESSAGE:
NAME:		
COMPANY:		
PHONE:		
EMAIL:		
IMPORTANCE: LOW ☐ MEDIUM ☐ HIGH ☐		CALLED ☐

DATE:	TIME:	MESSAGE:
NAME:		
COMPANY:		
PHONE:		
EMAIL:		
IMPORTANCE: LOW ☐ MEDIUM ☐ HIGH ☐		CALLED ☐

DATE: TIME:	MESSAGE:
NAME:	
COMPANY:	
PHONE:	
EMAIL:	
IMPORTANCE: LOW ☐ MEDIUM ☐ HIGH ☐	CALLED ☐
DATE: TIME:	MESSAGE:
NAME:	
COMPANY:	
PHONE:	
EMAIL:	
IMPORTANCE: LOW ☐ MEDIUM ☐ HIGH ☐	CALLED ☐
DATE: TIME:	MESSAGE:
NAME:	
COMPANY:	
PHONE:	
EMAIL:	
IMPORTANCE: LOW ☐ MEDIUM ☐ HIGH ☐	CALLED ☐
DATE: TIME:	MESSAGE:
NAME:	
COMPANY:	
PHONE:	
EMAIL:	
IMPORTANCE: LOW ☐ MEDIUM ☐ HIGH ☐	CALLED ☐
DATE: TIME:	MESSAGE:
NAME:	
COMPANY:	
PHONE:	
EMAIL:	
IMPORTANCE: LOW ☐ MEDIUM ☐ HIGH ☐	CALLED ☐

DATE:	TIME:	MESSAGE:
NAME:		
COMPANY:		
PHONE:		
EMAIL:		
IMPORTANCE: LOW ☐ MEDIUM ☐ HIGH ☐		CALLED ☐

DATE:	TIME:	MESSAGE:
NAME:		
COMPANY:		
PHONE:		
EMAIL:		
IMPORTANCE: LOW ☐ MEDIUM ☐ HIGH ☐		CALLED ☐

DATE:	TIME:	MESSAGE:
NAME:		
COMPANY:		
PHONE:		
EMAIL:		
IMPORTANCE: LOW ☐ MEDIUM ☐ HIGH ☐		CALLED ☐

DATE:	TIME:	MESSAGE:
NAME:		
COMPANY:		
PHONE:		
EMAIL:		
IMPORTANCE: LOW ☐ MEDIUM ☐ HIGH ☐		CALLED ☐

DATE:	TIME:	MESSAGE:
NAME:		
COMPANY:		
PHONE:		
EMAIL:		
IMPORTANCE: LOW ☐ MEDIUM ☐ HIGH ☐		CALLED ☐

DATE: **TIME:**	**MESSAGE:**
NAME:	
COMPANY:	
PHONE:	
EMAIL:	
IMPORTANCE: LOW ☐ **MEDIUM** ☐ **HIGH** ☐	**CALLED** ☐
DATE: **TIME:**	**MESSAGE:**
NAME:	
COMPANY:	
PHONE:	
EMAIL:	
IMPORTANCE: LOW ☐ **MEDIUM** ☐ **HIGH** ☐	**CALLED** ☐
DATE: **TIME:**	**MESSAGE:**
NAME:	
COMPANY:	
PHONE:	
EMAIL:	
IMPORTANCE: LOW ☐ **MEDIUM** ☐ **HIGH** ☐	**CALLED** ☐
DATE: **TIME:**	**MESSAGE:**
NAME:	
COMPANY:	
PHONE:	
EMAIL:	
IMPORTANCE: LOW ☐ **MEDIUM** ☐ **HIGH** ☐	**CALLED** ☐
DATE: **TIME:**	**MESSAGE:**
NAME:	
COMPANY:	
PHONE:	
EMAIL:	
IMPORTANCE: LOW ☐ **MEDIUM** ☐ **HIGH** ☐	**CALLED** ☐

DATE:　　　　**TIME:**	**MESSAGE:**
NAME:	
COMPANY:	
PHONE:	
EMAIL:	
IMPORTANCE: LOW ☐ **MEDIUM** ☐ **HIGH** ☐	**CALLED** ☐
DATE:　　　　**TIME:**	**MESSAGE:**
NAME:	
COMPANY:	
PHONE:	
EMAIL:	
IMPORTANCE: LOW ☐ **MEDIUM** ☐ **HIGH** ☐	**CALLED** ☐
DATE:　　　　**TIME:**	**MESSAGE:**
NAME:	
COMPANY:	
PHONE:	
EMAIL:	
IMPORTANCE: LOW ☐ **MEDIUM** ☐ **HIGH** ☐	**CALLED** ☐
DATE:　　　　**TIME:**	**MESSAGE:**
NAME:	
COMPANY:	
PHONE:	
EMAIL:	
IMPORTANCE: LOW ☐ **MEDIUM** ☐ **HIGH** ☐	**CALLED** ☐
DATE:　　　　**TIME:**	**MESSAGE:**
NAME:	
COMPANY:	
PHONE:	
EMAIL:	
IMPORTANCE: LOW ☐ **MEDIUM** ☐ **HIGH** ☐	**CALLED** ☐

DATE: **TIME:**	**MESSAGE:**
NAME:	
COMPANY:	
PHONE:	
EMAIL:	
IMPORTANCE: LOW ☐ **MEDIUM** ☐ **HIGH** ☐	**CALLED** ☐
DATE: **TIME:**	**MESSAGE:**
NAME:	
COMPANY:	
PHONE:	
EMAIL:	
IMPORTANCE: LOW ☐ **MEDIUM** ☐ **HIGH** ☐	**CALLED** ☐
DATE: **TIME:**	**MESSAGE:**
NAME:	
COMPANY:	
PHONE:	
EMAIL:	
IMPORTANCE: LOW ☐ **MEDIUM** ☐ **HIGH** ☐	**CALLED** ☐
DATE: **TIME:**	**MESSAGE:**
NAME:	
COMPANY:	
PHONE:	
EMAIL:	
IMPORTANCE: LOW ☐ **MEDIUM** ☐ **HIGH** ☐	**CALLED** ☐
DATE: **TIME:**	**MESSAGE:**
NAME:	
COMPANY:	
PHONE:	
EMAIL:	
IMPORTANCE: LOW ☐ **MEDIUM** ☐ **HIGH** ☐	**CALLED** ☐

DATE: **TIME:**	**MESSAGE:**
NAME:	
COMPANY:	
PHONE:	
EMAIL:	
IMPORTANCE: LOW ☐ **MEDIUM** ☐ **HIGH** ☐	**CALLED** ☐
DATE: **TIME:**	**MESSAGE:**
NAME:	
COMPANY:	
PHONE:	
EMAIL:	
IMPORTANCE: LOW ☐ **MEDIUM** ☐ **HIGH** ☐	**CALLED** ☐
DATE: **TIME:**	**MESSAGE:**
NAME:	
COMPANY:	
PHONE:	
EMAIL:	
IMPORTANCE: LOW ☐ **MEDIUM** ☐ **HIGH** ☐	**CALLED** ☐
DATE: **TIME:**	**MESSAGE:**
NAME:	
COMPANY:	
PHONE:	
EMAIL:	
IMPORTANCE: LOW ☐ **MEDIUM** ☐ **HIGH** ☐	**CALLED** ☐
DATE: **TIME:**	**MESSAGE:**
NAME:	
COMPANY:	
PHONE:	
EMAIL:	
IMPORTANCE: LOW ☐ **MEDIUM** ☐ **HIGH** ☐	**CALLED** ☐

DATE: TIME:	MESSAGE:
NAME:	
COMPANY:	
PHONE:	
EMAIL:	
IMPORTANCE: LOW ☐ MEDIUM ☐ HIGH ☐	CALLED ☐
DATE: TIME:	MESSAGE:
NAME:	
COMPANY:	
PHONE:	
EMAIL:	
IMPORTANCE: LOW ☐ MEDIUM ☐ HIGH ☐	CALLED ☐
DATE: TIME:	MESSAGE:
NAME:	
COMPANY:	
PHONE:	
EMAIL:	
IMPORTANCE: LOW ☐ MEDIUM ☐ HIGH ☐	CALLED ☐
DATE: TIME:	MESSAGE:
NAME:	
COMPANY:	
PHONE:	
EMAIL:	
IMPORTANCE: LOW ☐ MEDIUM ☐ HIGH ☐	CALLED ☐
DATE: TIME:	MESSAGE:
NAME:	
COMPANY:	
PHONE:	
EMAIL:	
IMPORTANCE: LOW ☐ MEDIUM ☐ HIGH ☐	CALLED ☐

DATE: **TIME:**	**MESSAGE:**
NAME:	
COMPANY:	
PHONE:	
EMAIL:	
IMPORTANCE: LOW ☐ **MEDIUM** ☐ **HIGH** ☐	**CALLED** ☐
DATE: **TIME:**	**MESSAGE:**
NAME:	
COMPANY:	
PHONE:	
EMAIL:	
IMPORTANCE: LOW ☐ **MEDIUM** ☐ **HIGH** ☐	**CALLED** ☐
DATE: **TIME:**	**MESSAGE:**
NAME:	
COMPANY:	
PHONE:	
EMAIL:	
IMPORTANCE: LOW ☐ **MEDIUM** ☐ **HIGH** ☐	**CALLED** ☐
DATE: **TIME:**	**MESSAGE:**
NAME:	
COMPANY:	
PHONE:	
EMAIL:	
IMPORTANCE: LOW ☐ **MEDIUM** ☐ **HIGH** ☐	**CALLED** ☐
DATE: **TIME:**	**MESSAGE:**
NAME:	
COMPANY:	
PHONE:	
EMAIL:	
IMPORTANCE: LOW ☐ **MEDIUM** ☐ **HIGH** ☐	**CALLED** ☐

DATE:	TIME:	MESSAGE:
NAME:		
COMPANY:		
PHONE:		
EMAIL:		
IMPORTANCE: LOW ☐ MEDIUM ☐ HIGH ☐		CALLED ☐

DATE:	TIME:	MESSAGE:
NAME:		
COMPANY:		
PHONE:		
EMAIL:		
IMPORTANCE: LOW ☐ MEDIUM ☐ HIGH ☐		CALLED ☐

DATE:	TIME:	MESSAGE:
NAME:		
COMPANY:		
PHONE:		
EMAIL:		
IMPORTANCE: LOW ☐ MEDIUM ☐ HIGH ☐		CALLED ☐

DATE:	TIME:	MESSAGE:
NAME:		
COMPANY:		
PHONE:		
EMAIL:		
IMPORTANCE: LOW ☐ MEDIUM ☐ HIGH ☐		CALLED ☐

DATE:	TIME:	MESSAGE:
NAME:		
COMPANY:		
PHONE:		
EMAIL:		
IMPORTANCE: LOW ☐ MEDIUM ☐ HIGH ☐		CALLED ☐

DATE:	TIME:	MESSAGE:
NAME:		
COMPANY:		
PHONE:		
EMAIL:		
IMPORTANCE: LOW ☐ **MEDIUM** ☐ **HIGH** ☐		**CALLED** ☐

DATE:	TIME:	MESSAGE:
NAME:		
COMPANY:		
PHONE:		
EMAIL:		
IMPORTANCE: LOW ☐ **MEDIUM** ☐ **HIGH** ☐		**CALLED** ☐

DATE:	TIME:	MESSAGE:
NAME:		
COMPANY:		
PHONE:		
EMAIL:		
IMPORTANCE: LOW ☐ **MEDIUM** ☐ **HIGH** ☐		**CALLED** ☐

DATE:	TIME:	MESSAGE:
NAME:		
COMPANY:		
PHONE:		
EMAIL:		
IMPORTANCE: LOW ☐ **MEDIUM** ☐ **HIGH** ☐		**CALLED** ☐

DATE:	TIME:	MESSAGE:
NAME:		
COMPANY:		
PHONE:		
EMAIL:		
IMPORTANCE: LOW ☐ **MEDIUM** ☐ **HIGH** ☐		**CALLED** ☐

DATE:	TIME:	MESSAGE:
NAME:		
COMPANY:		
PHONE:		
EMAIL:		
IMPORTANCE: LOW ▢ MEDIUM ▢ HIGH ▢		CALLED ▢

DATE:	TIME:	MESSAGE:
NAME:		
COMPANY:		
PHONE:		
EMAIL:		
IMPORTANCE: LOW ▢ MEDIUM ▢ HIGH ▢		CALLED ▢

DATE:	TIME:	MESSAGE:
NAME:		
COMPANY:		
PHONE:		
EMAIL:		
IMPORTANCE: LOW ▢ MEDIUM ▢ HIGH ▢		CALLED ▢

DATE:	TIME:	MESSAGE:
NAME:		
COMPANY:		
PHONE:		
EMAIL:		
IMPORTANCE: LOW ▢ MEDIUM ▢ HIGH ▢		CALLED ▢

DATE:	TIME:	MESSAGE:
NAME:		
COMPANY:		
PHONE:		
EMAIL:		
IMPORTANCE: LOW ▢ MEDIUM ▢ HIGH ▢		CALLED ▢

DATE: TIME:	MESSAGE:
NAME:	
COMPANY:	
PHONE:	
EMAIL:	
IMPORTANCE: LOW ☐ **MEDIUM** ☐ **HIGH** ☐	**CALLED** ☐

DATE: TIME:	MESSAGE:
NAME:	
COMPANY:	
PHONE:	
EMAIL:	
IMPORTANCE: LOW ☐ **MEDIUM** ☐ **HIGH** ☐	**CALLED** ☐

DATE: TIME:	MESSAGE:
NAME:	
COMPANY:	
PHONE:	
EMAIL:	
IMPORTANCE: LOW ☐ **MEDIUM** ☐ **HIGH** ☐	**CALLED** ☐

DATE: TIME:	MESSAGE:
NAME:	
COMPANY:	
PHONE:	
EMAIL:	
IMPORTANCE: LOW ☐ **MEDIUM** ☐ **HIGH** ☐	**CALLED** ☐

DATE: TIME:	MESSAGE:
NAME:	
COMPANY:	
PHONE:	
EMAIL:	
IMPORTANCE: LOW ☐ **MEDIUM** ☐ **HIGH** ☐	**CALLED** ☐

Made in the USA
Columbia, SC
22 July 2024

39143246R00067